ABSTRACT

The terrorist attacks of 9/11 caused Americans to realize that our sense of invincibility had been shattered. This paper will identify Al-Qa'ida and *Salafi-Jihadists* as our enemy and will recommend new approaches to fighting terrorism. I will explore Al-Qa'ida's organization, leaders, doctrine and their radical ideologies. I will argue that the war we must fight is one against Islamist transnational actors who openly engage in terrorism or support terrorism. I will highlight that our current National and Military Strategies to combat terrorism are inadequate to take on an ideologically emboldened transnational foe. I will emphasize that we must refocus our efforts and prepare to fight a war of several generations (long war) and will recommend several initiatives to include development of a cogent Grand National Strategy. These recommendations are intended to assist future planners in the development of a Grand National Strategy and an integrated long war campaign plan aimed directly at Al-Qa'ida, the Al-Qa'ida Associated Movement, and Islamist terrorists and executed through the application of diplomatic, informational, military and economic instruments of national power by an unified interagency effort in coordination with our multinational partners, international governmental and non-governmental organizations and regional security organizations.

The Serpent in Our Garden: Al-Qa'ida and The Long War

Terrorism has existed for centuries and governments have struggled to counter the violent extremist threat within their midst. In the immediate days following the unprovoked attacks against the United States on September 11, 2001, President Bush and our collective national leaders stressed the urgent need to go on the immediate offensive against the terrorists, deploy military forces, and promote democracy abroad. Now, going on seven years in the Global War on Terror (GWOT), one can argue we have made credible tactical gains, but have fallen far short in defeating violent extremism as a threat to our way of life. Cooperation amongst the international community has resulted in genuine security improvements – particularly in disruption of terrorist organizations and finances, securing of borders with tighter security at points of entry, and the killing or capture of individuals of high value. We have seen greater cooperation amongst many countries and internally within the United States, among the interagency to include some specific reforms. But, despite these successes, significant challenges remain and terror organizations like Al-Qa'ida have adapted, are conducting transnational irregular warfare and have grown stronger and more widespread then before the attacks of 9/11.[1] The most recent National Intelligence Estimate judges that the U.S. homeland will continue to face a persistent and evolving terrorist threat, mainly from Islamic terrorist groups and cells and that Al-Qa'ida will remain the most serious threat.[2] More important, the current administration's approach to the war on terror has created more terrorists than it has eliminated and that anti-American sentiment across the world and throughout the Middle East has skyrocketed serving to fuel and inspire Muslims to join or openly support terror groups. I believe we have failed to understand the true enemy who opposes us, the allure and appeal that they hold for the people of Islam worldwide, and our misguided efforts at engaging in a "war of ideas" have been clearly one-sided and not in our favor. Without a clear concept of what victory in a war on terror should look like, we will exhaust our resources to include our service men and women in futility.

Our near enemy, Al-Qa'ida has been engaging in war for nearly four decades in order to achieve their overall strategic objective of a world-wide Islamic caliphate where the only law is *shar'ia* (Islamic law). Al-Qa'ida continues to evolve, has increased its global reach and appeal, and has inspired numerous other extremist groups while continuing to expand its worldwide network. Al-Qa'ida has been elevated to the status we would hold for an institution, not just the world's most feared terrorist group. But they are neither invincible nor invulnerable, and they have stumbled momentously more than once.

Today, our heroic military forces have fought tremendously and garnered numerous significant results and tactical victories on the operational fronts in Afghanistan, Iraq, the Philippines and Northeast (HORN) of Africa, some of which are clearly irreversible gains. We have also gained greater insight into this elusive organization and now understand some of the cracks or fissures within their foundation. This newly found understanding and comprehension by experts in the field of study of terrorism, as well as our national leaders, has enlightened us to the simple fact that we must prepare to wage a long war against the Al-Qa'ida Associated Movement (AQAM) and Islamist terrorism. A war that will incorporate all elements of national power in a cogent and executable strategy as well as build and leverage multinational partnerships.

A war where the United States is well resourced but, at present, ill-prepared to lead and to conduct.

This strategic research project will concentrate on terrorism both past present and future, and will thoroughly examine Al-Qa'ida, the correct adversary, and how to counter them with the development of a Grand National Strategy and long war approach. I will highlight Al-Qa'ida history and evolution over time, their structure, leaders, doctrine and their radically motivated ideology within the context of greater Islam and Political Islamists (Islamism) and *Sunni* fundamentalist ideologies. Al-Qa'ida is leveraging an ongoing internal struggle within Islam that is not about liberation, but about revival of the religion and a part of a larger Islamic social movement. We are not at war with Islam, but will need to wage war against organizations that use terror as a primary means in order to achieve their desired ends, cloak themselves and use Islam as justification for their actions, and that these organizations are a direct threat against our core national security interests as well as those of our friends and partners world-wide. I will argue that the war we must fight is not a global war against terrorism, but a war against select transnational actors or states that overtly or covertly support terrorism, within the global arena context and through new forms of warfare. I will highlight that our current National and Military Strategies to combat terrorism are inadequate to take on an ideological emboldened transnational foe, Al-Qa'ida and the movement they inspire. I will emphasize that we must reassess, reprioritize and refocus our efforts, and prepare to fight a war of several decades, or quite possibly several generations (long war). To better prepare in waging the long war, I will recommend several initiatives to include development of a cogent Grand National Strategy against

Islamist terror organizations that identifies attainable objectives (strategic ends), allowing us to clearly envision victory and under what conditions. My recommendations will not eliminate terror in the world, but are intended to assist future strategic and operational planners as well as policy makers in the development of a much needed Grand National Strategy. A Grand National Strategy and comprehensive and Integrated Long War Campaign Plan (ILWCP) aimed directly at Al-Qa'ida, the Al-Qa'ida Associated Movement, Islamist terrorists (*Jihadis*) and executed through the combined and coordinated application of diplomatic, informational, military, and economic instruments of national power supported by a cohesive unified interagency effort in coordination with our multinational partners, various international governmental and non-governmental organizations and regional security organizations.

Terrorism

Terrorism implies indiscriminate violence, panic, brutality, and evil. To label a group as a terrorist group or an individual as a terrorist, we seek to imply that the group or individual is immoral, or acts contrary to basic ethical principles. Terrorists attack governments that are legitimate and they seek to undermine or destroy a political system or even a way of life.[3] It is no surprise that there are multiple definitions of terrorism, many complex, and some simple. Defining terrorism has proven exceptionally difficult, thus policy makers, government agencies, countries as well as scholars have no agreed upon definition. For the purpose of this research project the definition used throughout this work is one derived from the works of Kushner, Claridge, and Hoffman who approached terrorism from different perspectives, but between them address the key ingredients involved.

Terrorism involves political aims and motives. It is violent or threatens violence and it is designed to generate fear in a target audience that extends beyond the immediate victims of the violence. The violence is conducted by identifiable organizations, which are either non-state or state actors as perpetrators. Finally the acts of violence are intended to create power in situations in which power was previously lacking (i.e. the violence attempts to enhance the power base of the organization undertaking the organizations – to increase the probability of being able to influence political decisions, and to achieve the organizations goals).[4]

Terrorism is not a new phenomenon or method of warfare and can be traced back to when medieval rulers hired assassins to murder political opponents. Terrorism is meant to deliberately create and exploit fear, in order to attain political objectives and change. It is undeniably a form of psychological warfare and is meant to instill fear and have far reaching psychological effects beyond the target audience of immediate victims of an attack.[5] Governments and states have lived and dealt with terrorist groups for centuries, but with the evolution of science and technology in the past fifty years to include commercial air travel, the new media explosion and the internet, new forms of terrorist activity have occurred that can instantaneously reach global audiences.[6] The modern news media and World Wide Web remains the principal conduit of information for terrorist groups and acts, and both are vital components that facilitate terror groups' ability to affect their larger targeted audiences. As a result of the explosion of the World Wide Web, terrorist organizations have expanded their propaganda and information efforts and now control the communication process by determining content, context, and over which mediums their message is projected toward the multiple audiences they desire to influence.[7] Modern day terrorists' measure success not by conventional warfare accepted metrics (body counts, amount of military assets destroyed or geography seized) but, rather the amount of attention they have attracted to their cause and by the psychological impact and effects they hope to exert over the target audience.[8]

To effectively fight terror in the 21st century, we must first look back and understand how *modern terrorism* has evolved throughout history. UCLA professor, David Rapoport, describes four clear waves of **modern terror** throughout history and how certain technology improvements have fostered evolutionary change. In the 1880s, the "*Anarchist Wave*" appeared and lasted some forty years. Its successor, the "*Anti-Colonial Wave*" began in the 1920s and then largely disappeared by the mid-1960s. The birth of the "*New Left Wave*" grew out of the late 1960s and dissipated in the 1990s, leaving a few terror groups still active in Sri Lanka, Spain, France, Peru, and Columbia. The fourth wave, the "*Religious Wave*" exploded onto the scene with the Iranian Revolution of 1979, and if past precedent holds true will have another twenty to thirty years to run its course before a fifth wave appears.[9] The *first wave* of modern terrorism began in the late 19th century, largely due to doctrine and technology and transformation of communication and transportation patterns. Where America became directly involved with modern terror was an outcome of failure in Vietnam, which many perceived that the effectiveness of Vietcong against the American Goliath armed with a huge technological advantage, inspired hope that the West was vulnerable.[10] In the *third wave*, radicalism and nationalism were often combined. Groups like the American Weather Underground, Italian Red Brigades, French Action Directe, and Basque Separatists viewed themselves of leading the vanguard of violent political activism. Airline hijacking and embassy attacks, as well as high profile kidnappings (409 kidnappings – 951 hostages taken from 1968 – 1982),[11] were the tactics of choice. As revolutionary terrorists were defeated in country after country and the *third wave* ebbed, the *fourth wave* exploded with the Iranian Revolution and fall of the Shah of Iran. Islam is the most important religion in this wave and with the success of the overthrow of the Shah, inspired other Islamic terror movements in Iraq, Saudi Arabia, Lebanon, and Kuwait. Two important factors started with the *fourth wave*: the introduction of suicide bombing or self-martyrdom, introduced by Shiites in Lebanon, and American military presence in the Middle East region. Assassinations and kidnapping persisted in the current wave of modern terror, but suicide bombing was the most radical and prolific tactic. Terror groups during this period focused primarily towards large scale attacks on military and government installations.[12]

The European Unions Terrorism Working Party (TWP) has systematically tracked and analyzed terror acts and groups across the member nations, and presents their findings annually to the European Parliament. The TWPs categorization by major type of terrorist organization is widely accepted by other agencies when tracking terror acts back to groups and motivations. The four major groups of terrorist organizations are: 1) Left-Wing and Anarchist Groups, 2) Right-Wing Groups, 3) Islamist Terror Groups, and 4) Ethno-Nationalist and Separatist Groups.[13] This research project will focus primarily on the most dangerous group. The group that is a clear and present danger to our national security and way of life, Islamist terrorism.

Terrorist groups do not rise randomly; there must be motive and intent (political ends) as well as a common belief or ideology that binds individuals together that commit acts of terror. Over the past forty years of research a common theme suggests that terrorist attacks are a product of two primary elements, motivation and capabilities.[14] But a more comprehensive analysis must be undertaken, one that considers the ideologies and leaders-scholars that influence terrorist groups, as well as socio-political dynamics of terrorist objectives and the social dynamics of the people they draw their support from in order for researchers to clearly understand all the motivators of why terror groups come into being.

Poor living conditions, socioeconomic factors as well as political repression are often the motivation for individuals to join terror groups or cells but, are not the only reasons. The Islamic based terror groups we face today have gained in number and capacity because of four major root causes:

1) Political repression within Islamic governments that have close relationships with the United States.

2) Lack of monetary financial sharing within Islamic states. The elites maintain the wealth (the masses are economically repressed).

3) Resentment of the West due to the perceived exploitation of Islamic countries primarily by the United States.

4) The increasing credibility gap between Muslims (primarily in the Middle East) and the United States.

The majority of individuals and groups that become motivated to pursue terrorism do so because they envision and long for a future that they believe will not materialize unless they revert to violence. The perception of the United States as a primary adversary, (us versus them), is an underlying stream that has given rise to anti-American sentiment and providing incentive for Islamist based terrorist groups. Islamist terrorism gained prominence and rose over other terror groups during the decline of leftist ideology, and Islamists used their religion as the vehicle for dissent. The Soviet-Afghan War helped to stimulate and then elevate Islamic Terrorism to the forefront in three major ways:

1) Provided skills and experience to Arabs and Afghan fighters who came to wage in *Jihad.*

2) The ultimate network for extremism arose during this opportunity to wage war as *mujahidin*, against the Soviets (*Jihadi's* come to Afghanistan to fight).

3) The lesson that violence can win (defeat of the Soviet regime and Afghan Najibullah regime which fell in 1992).[15]

The ultimate victory of the Afghan *mujahidin*, aided by their Arab brothers who joined them in battle, and the 1979 Iranian revolution led by Ayatollah Khomeini against the Shah of Iran, were symbolic victories that provided future *Jihadis* the proof that weaker groups committed to a cause that was just, could topple more powerful regimes despite overwhelming odds.[16]

Since the 9/11 attacks, the nature of Islamist terrorism has become increasingly varied and more complex. Islamist terror organizations are more secretive, compartmentalized, and difficult to comprehend as terrorism continues to evolve both as a tactic and a strategy. Military response has been marginally effective against today's terrorists, but will not be effective against tomorrow's. Western response to terrorism and the attacks of 9/11 has been reactive or event-driven and we must progress towards a campaign and objectives driven strategy in order to have a reasonable chance of winning. Effectiveness against terrorism cannot be measured in terms of the numbers of terrorists killed or captured (such as war and violent crime), but rather our ability to counter the psychological impact and political effects.

Brian Michael Jenkins, noted terrorist scholar who has researched and written on terrorism since the late 1970s, holds the following observations in the new age of terrorism:

- Terrorism has become bloodier, more violent, and more lethal.

- Terrorist groups have developed new and innovative ways for financial support, thus becoming less-dependant on state sponsors.

- New models of organization are evolving and continue to adapt.

- Terror campaigns are becoming more global, due to technology, the internet and globalization.

- Terrorists are effectively exploiting new communications technologies.[17]

Although his observations are relevant and important to analyze in order to determine trends, patterns, and most important vulnerabilities, they do not afford a looking glass for accurate prediction of future terrorist attacks. Looking back over the past twenty-five years, it is unlikely that we could have accurately predicted the current state of terror groups in the world today and that the United States would be in the midst of waging a global war against terrorism. However, it is extraordinarily important that we comprehend how much more sophisticated terror groups will become and how local, regional and transnational terror groups will achieve greater interconnectivity, thus achieving greater overall effects. A dynamic that is a direct result of the movement inspired by Al-Qa'ida and its core leadership.

<u>Al-Qa'ida, Jihadis, Salafis, Islamists and Islamic Fundamentalism</u>

Al-Qa'ida is arguably the first multinational terrorist group in this century that also presents an apocalyptic threat to the world order. The Al-Qa'ida Associated Movement (AQAM) is a global network of Islamist terrorists groups capable of mobilization and escalation of conflict to unimagined levels and has moved terrorism beyond an instrument of violent political activism, to compete with and challenge Western power and influence in the Middle East.[18] Founded in 1987, by Palestine-Jordanian ideologue Abdullah Yusuf Azzam (mentor of Osama Bin Laden), it evolved out of the remaining Arab fighters and veterans of the war against the Soviet Union in Afghanistan.[19] Bin Laden and Azzam cofounded the *Maktab al Khidmat lil Mujahidin al-Arab* (MAK, or Afghan Service Bureau) in Peshawar, Pakistan in 1984. Together, they disseminated propaganda, raised funds and recruited members through networks worldwide, to include the United States. The MAK housed, trained, financed, and fought the anti-Soviet Afghan *Jihad* (holy war), ultimately succeeding and expelling Soviet forces from Afghanistan. Azzam envisioned the redirection of the *mujahidin* (holy warriors of God) into an ideologically motivated group, empowered to come to the aid of Muslims worldwide.[20] Azzam, then the spiritual leader of international Islamists everywhere, established the founding guidelines for training Al-Qa'ida, which he saw as a secretive, pious group and pioneering vanguard of holy warriors. As the Soviet *Jihad* culminated with the defeat of the "evil Soviet empire," many fighters were zealously driven to precipitate radical change in certain Arab social and political societies. In order to engage successfully in conflicts involving Muslims, Al-Qa'ida established ideological, financial, military, and political influence over several Islamist terror groups. As the group was establishing itself on an international level, Azzam was assassinated in

Peshawar in November 1989, many believe this was sanctioned and due to the influence of Ayman al-Zawahiri on Osama bin Laden. With Azzam out of the picture, this clearly ended the irrevocable split between Bin Laden and his former mentor and professor, and bin Laden would be the driving influence behind the future path for Al-Qa'ida. Azzam had advocated the traditional fundamentalist interpretation of the nature of *Jihad*; the reclaiming of once Muslim lands from non-Muslim rulers in places like Palestine and southern Spain. The militants who supported bin Laden advocated a much more radical approach, the violent overthrow of governments across the Middle East of which they claimed were "apostate" and repressive.[21] Osama Bin Laden would soon emerge as the modern face of terror, and leader of a much larger *Jihadi* movement. It is now imperative to understand how Al-Qa'ida fits within the larger continuum of *Salafi-Jihadi* and Islamist movements.

Ideology within Islam

The Combating Terror Center (CTC) at West Point, New York, provides a useful framework with which to better understand the *Jihadi* movement within greater Islam. They situate the *Jihadi* movement within the various Muslim constituencies that *Jihadi* leaders target to persuade and influence. The variety of constituencies is best envisioned in a series of nesting circles (Figure 1: Jihadi Constituencies).

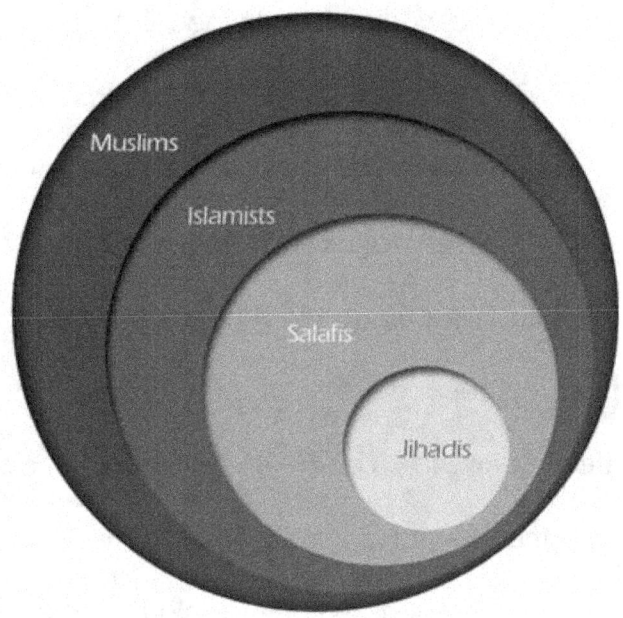

Figure 1. Jihadi Constituencies[22]

Each constituency is responds to the leadership in the broader constituencies of which they are a part of, but each also has its own internal ideologues or thinkers which are situated to best influence their base. The largest group is comprised of Muslims, those who are followers of the *Qur'an,* teachings of the Prophet Muhammad, and the *Sunnah-Hadith* (source of Islamic doctrine).[23] This group includes the *Sunnis* (those who follow examples of the Prophet) and *Shi'is* (those who follow the Prophet and the descendants through his son-in-law, Ali), the *Sufis (*mystics who formed brotherhoods and added idol worship to the practice of Islam), and range from secularist to fundamentalist groups. The group is so enormous that no one or two scholars or ideologues shape opinion across the broader spectrum of individuals.[24]

Islamists, Muslims who want Islamic law (*shari'a*) to be the primary source of law and cultural identity within the state, comprise the next smaller group. They differ to some extent on the meaning of this idea and over how to achieve their goals. Among the *Sunnis* (largest majority of the world's Islamic peoples), the Muslim Brotherhood is the most influential group, with Yusuf Qaradawi as their most influential spokesman.[25]

Salafis are *Sunni* Muslims who want to establish and govern Islamic states based solely on the first generation of interpretation of the teachings of the Prophet and the *Qu'ran,* and to abandon modern secular governments. However, *Salafis* diverge with respect to the final form of the desired states and the proper methods of achieving a unified collection of states (caliphate). The *Salafi* movement is closest ideologically to the Puritan movement in America and England. The Saudi clerics are the most influential *Salafis.*[26] *Salafi* movement draw their theology primarily from the *Hanbali* school of Islam. The movement has also attracted the more militant and radical of Islamists.

The Holy Warriors or *Jihadis* are today's most recognized terrorists and are a part of the greater *Salafi* movement. *Jihadi* thinkers draw legitimacy for their actions from the *Salafist* ideology. The most influential present day thinkers that are influencing the *Salafi-Jihadis are*:

1) Abu Muhammad al-Maqdisi (Jordanian-Palestinian writer), best known as the spiritual mentor of Jordanian born terrorist, Abu Musab al-Zarqawi. Al-Maqdisi is currently in the custody of the Jordanian government, but curiously runs and maintains the main Al-Qa'ida internet site (*Tawhed*) of pro terrorism *Jihadist* ideological readings.[27] Through his writings on *Tawhed*, al-Maqdisi attempts to set the agenda for a variety of *mujahidin* groups to follow as they enter into *Jihad*.

2) Abu Basir al-Tartusi, another prolific modern scholar from Syria, who is slightly more moderate and lives in London. He has provided scholarly arguments to legitimize

armed resistance against tyrannical rule, or employ *Jihadi* tactics, while living in accordance with *shari'a* law.[28]

3) Abu Qatada al-Filistini, born in 1960 in the West Bank, now living in England. Al-Filistini is an example of a cleric who encourages *Jihad* against apostate rule in accordance with the *shari'a*. His writings contend that it is every Muslim's individual obligation to overthrow and expel any secular government from Muslim lands through violent means (bombings, sabotage or terror) to advance the implementation of the *shari'a*. He is alleged to be a member of Al-Qa'ida's *Fatwa* Committee, but is currently fighting extradition to Jordan.[29]

4) 'Abd al-Qadir bin 'Abd al-'Aziz, born in 1950 in Upper Egypt. After serving in Peshewar with other *Jihadis*, he founded and became the first leader of al-Jihad al-Islami fir Misr (Islamic Jihad in Egypt), until Dr. Zawahiri took over in 1991. Indications exist that al-Zawahiri published some of al-Qadir's writings under his own name, and therefore likely split over this controversy. Al-Qadir authored *"Rislat al 'umda fi l'dad al-udda li'l-jihad fi sabil allah"*, an important *Jihad* manual which numerous terrorist cells have embraced.[30]

5) Noted Saudi Clerics who use *Salafi* teachings in their mosques or in writings to inspire *Jihad* amongst the Muslim communities.

These individuals possess significant influence on *Jihadi* organizations and they are also in the best position to condemn violence, and denounce *Jihadi* organizations that revert to terror to achieve their aims. Denouncements of prominent *Jihadis* by other prominent *Jihadis* or ideologues is extremely damaging and often demoralizing.[31]

It is important to understand that Al-Qa'ida draws upon both modern day and historical writers and scholars to fashion their ideological messages. The most influential medieval and modern day Muslim authors were largely scholars known for their rigid interpretations of the *Qu'ran*. *Jihadis* develop their militant interpretations of the *shari'a* and Islamist theology, by narrowing their delineations of proper Islamic beliefs and practices.[32] Additional noteworthy thinkers who have influenced Al-Qa'ida and *Salafi-Jihadis* are:

1) Ibn Taymiyya (born 1263 in Harran - present day Turkey, died 1328). The most influential scholar of the late Hanbali school of Islam. A widely prolific writer and often cited polemic of the *Salafi* movement who was extremely critical of the *Sufis*.[33] His writings are considered omnipotent in that they laid the foundations to justify fighting *Jihad* against foreign invaders (an Al-Qa'ida core theme).

2) Ibn 'Abd al-Wahhab (born 1703 in Saudi Arabia, died 1792). Wahhab's writings were dedicated to the purification of Islam from the innovations or idolatry worships that had over time corrupted Islam from its inception - the struggle to return to the ways and beliefs of Islam's "pious forbearers". The Kingdom of Saudi Arabia was founded upon the 18th century *Wahhabisim* reform movement, and is the prominent form of Islam within the Kingdom and Qatar.

3) Sayyid Qutb (born in Egypt 1906, died 1966). Having worked in education and studied in the United States, he joined the Muslim Brotherhood and began to articulate through writing a militant anti-modernist within the context of early Islamic interpretation. Qutb is credited with establishing the discourse for *Salafi* and *Salafi-Jihadi* doctrines. Qutb believed that because of the lack of *shari'a* law the Islamic world was no longer

Muslim, and to restore Islam, a vanguard movement of pious Muslims was needed to rid the world of all non-Islamic influences, such as concepts like nationalism and socialism. Following his execution, he achieved martyrdom status which served as a catalyst for widespread growth of the Muslim Brotherhood and other modern Islamist political movements. His narrow interpretation of a true "Islamic identity" helped establish *Takfir*, or excommunication.[34]

The scholars and ideologues mentioned above have played a pivotal role in the greater *Jihadi* movement that is not widely understood and often overlooked by the West when developing policy or strategies in the current war on terrorism. The writings of these scholars, of which are their personal interpretations of the *Qu'ran* and *Sunnah*, are what are weaved into the stream of *Jihadi* ideology and violent rhetoric that binds the core Al-Qa'ida organization together along with creating strategic links across the wider Al-Qa'ida movement and amongst terror groups. Dr. Ayman al-Zawahiri (born 1951 in Egypt), a former surgeon and current deputy and theoretician to bin Laden, is often portrayed as the current brains of the *Jihadi* movement, but is a relatively insignificant theologian when compared against the aforementioned writers and Ideologues. In December 2001, he published the work "*Knights under the Prophet's Banner,*" extolling Al-Qa'ida's strategy which draws from all of the above scholars prominent works (most notably Qutb) and outlines a coherent framework of his interpretation of *Jihad*. Both al-Zawahiri and bin Laden are atypical of modern terrorists in that they both come from educated and well-to-do families, demonstrating the ideological appeal of Al-Qa'ida to all strata of Muslim society.[35]

The *Jihadi* movement can be described as an informal network of *Sunni* Muslims which desire to overthrow secular states and replace them with theocracies.[36] Like *takfir*, other strands of Islamic history and theology have proven useful to *Jihadi* groups. For example, *bay'a*, an oath of loyalty to Muhammad required of his followers, has often been used by *Jihadis* to tighten alliances among different groups.[37] What the West has yet to fully comprehend is that the *Jihadi* movement is not an aberration of Islam but, is a movement integral and born within Islam. The modern-day *Jihadi* movement has emerged from both historical conflict but also recent conflicts of Islamists with secular Arab governments to include a very strong connection between radical Egyptian Islamism and Al-Qa'ida. Islamists perceive that all Muslims have suffered at the expense of the Western industrialized world and actively voice that Islam is under siege, which fuels radical and fundamentalist ideology. While Islamic fundamentalism has been brewing for centuries, it will continue to thrive as long as Jerusalem is contested, Muslims perceive Islam is threatened by outsiders or "infidels" and radicals are allowed to preach violent rhetoric, brainwashing millions through mosques and *madrassas* worldwide. While a fundamentalist may also be labeled an Islamist, an Islamic fundamentalist is a "political individual" in search of a return to original Islam.[38]

At the core of many extremist Islamic fundamentalists we can find a transformation of hatred into idealized love towards the Prophet, through Islam and the submission of self to the religion.[39] It is upon these individuals that Al-Qa'ida preys, encouraging these Muslims to join the greater *Jihadi* movement as holy warriors, often through self-martyrdom. But the *Jihadis* are vulnerable with regards to the true meaning of *Jihad* according to the *Qu'ran* and other Islamic doctrine, if America chooses to fight the war of ideas like a real war.

Schools of Islam and Sources of Islamic Doctrine.

Understanding the different schools and sects of Islam as well as the major sources of Islamic doctrine are important when developing counter-strategies to the radical and extremist ideologies of Islamic fundamentalists.

1) *Sunni* Muslims. Muslims who follow *Shafi, Hanifa, Malik,* and *Hanbali* schools. *Sunnis* approximately 83% of all Muslims and are considered to be main stream or traditionalists.

- *Maliki Madhab* School. Imam Malik was born in Medin, and this school of Sunni thought is most prevalent in North, Central, and West Africa.

- *Hanafi Madhab* School. Founded by Imam Abu Hanifa, out of Iraq. Most prominent in the Arab Middle East and South Asia.

- *Shafi'i Madhab* School. Imam Shafi'i inspired but also taught by Abu Hanifa and Imam Malik. Prominent in East Africa.

- *Hanbal Madhab* School. Originated in Baghdad, under Imam Ahmad ibn Hanbal who studied under Imam Shafi'i. Most prominent in Saudi Arabia and the Persian Gulf region. Closely mirrors *Wahhabi* doctrine.[40]

All four Sunni schools have numerous similarities, but differ in their finer interpretations, mainly due to each founder's individual interpretations of Islamic doctrine.

2) *Shi'a* Muslims. Followers of the *Jafari* school of Islam and comprise only 15% of all Muslims. *Shi'as* split from the *Sunnis* over the dispute on who is the rightful

successor to the Prophet Muhammad. *Shi'as* strictly interpret the *Qu'ran* and believe in the twelve Imams and that the 12th Imam has gone into hiding and will reappear in the future when certain conditions are met.[41]

       3) *Sufi* Muslims. A small minority, about 1% of all Muslims, who generally believe in the mystical interpretations within Islam to include Idolatry worship. Followers, formed in brotherhoods, believe God will speak to them directly through the practice of dance, and mysticism.[42]

       There are two major and two lesser sources of Islamic Doctrine that Muslim scholars, clerics, and people draw from. The major sources are the *Holy Qu'ran*, the *Sunnah-Hadith* (a collection of recorded sayings by the Prophet after his death). The minor doctrinal works are *Qiyas*, or analogies within Islam, and *Ijma*, general consensus amongst clerics and religious scholars.[43] Lastly, a final influencer is each Muslim's personal interpretation and understanding of all of the above.

       Latter-day and modern-day *Jihadi* writers have used Islamic doctrine in conjunction with select schools of *Sunni* Islam to develop their own radical ideologies and writings. An important learning point is that all emerging writers and authors who inspire today's *Jihadis* have developed rhetoric either directly or indirectly from Islamic doctrine. This is one major reason why their rhetoric appeals to the larger Muslim audience. It is also why Al-Qa'ida appeals to those who are disenfranchised with their own situation and each individual's perception of the current state of Islam.

Al-Qa'ida (The Base) and the Attacks of 9/11

       Even from the beginning in the aftermath of the *mujahidin* anti-Soviet *Jihad* in Afghanistan, Al-Qa'ida has struggled and has been at war with itself. The struggle emerged out of two factions, one committed to manning and equipping an effective guerilla organization and the other intent on establishing Al-Qa'ida as a movement and global brand - a battle standard that could be taken up by any group involved in Islamic resistance.[44] Ultimately, bin Laden prevailed as Al-Qa'ida moved forward towards a globally recognized transnational terrorist entity. Notwithstanding internal disagreements remained amongst the elites within his *Shura* Council over bin Ladens direction.

Osama bin Laden was born in Riyadh, Saudi Arabia, in 1957 to a wealthy and highly respected Arab family. His father was a favorite of the Saudi King Saud and his family had close ties with the Saudi royal family. By the time of his fathers death in a helicopter crash at the age of eleven, it was estimated Osama inherited between eighty and three hundred million dollars (U.S.).[45] It was during his time at King Abdul Aziz University in Jeddah, where he studied under Professor Abdullah Yusuf Azzam, that he was introduced to Islamism.[46] Both he and Azzam would eventually leave Jeddah and travel to Peshawar, and then fight in the Soviet-Afghan War. After the Soviets were defeated and withdrew, Arab fighters, under the command of bin Laden, took part in the siege of Jalalabad, which ultimately became a senseless bloodbath for his men and highlighted his tactical ineptness. The failure to win the battle of Jalalabad in 1989 set the stage for a war of attrition between the Afghan communist regime and the Arab and Afghan *mujahidin* fighters. It would take until April 1992, with the final fall of Kabul before ultimate success by the *mujahidin* in Afghanistan was achieved.[47]

After Afghanistan, bin Laden returned to Saudi Arabia, and was witness to Saddam Hussein's Iraqi Armed Forces invasion of Kuwait in 1990. Upon the occupation of Kuwait, the valuable Saudi oilfields were easily within easy striking distance of Iraqi units. Bin Laden offered King Fahd his *mujahidin* veterans to protect the country, but was refused and the King opted to allow U.S. forces and other allies to deploy on Saudi land. Bin Laden was greatly angered and after speaking out publicly, was quickly exiled to Sudan with his citizenship revoked. His hatred for his native country and its ruling elite would remain a constant fire within him for many years to come.

From 1992 – 1996, the bin Laden led Al-Qa'ida "central" operated from Sudan under the protection of the radical Islamic regime in Khartoum, until massive international pressure on the Sudanese Government caused them to expel both Al-Qa'ida and the Egyptian Islamic Jihad (EIJ). But it was during this time that Al-Qa'ida would first gain international recognition as a byproduct of the failure of the United States efforts in Somalia, where Al-Qa'ida played a noteworthy role.

Somalia is one of the world's poorest and least developed countries and much of their suffering has been by their own hands. In 1969, General Mohammed Siad Barre seized power during a military coup, aligned himself with the Soviet bloc countries for military arms, and would engender a repressive and corrupt regime.[48] In the late 1980s, various clans arose and violently opposed the Barre regime, ultimately overthrowing it in 1991, plunging the country into chaos. Fiefdoms arose from the ashes, where rival warlords battled openly and the country plummeted into a violent civil war. By late 1992, the war-town country had become a huge humanitarian crisis and unofficial reports indicated that close to 300,000 Somalis had died due to starvation, disease, or violence.[49] The United Nations Security Council authorized an emergency humanitarian mission in August of 1992, but due to deteriorating security relief efforts, was hindered and supplies were often plundered by warlords. To rescue this operation, President

George H. Bush ordered the Pentagon on December 9, 1992, to undertake OPERATION RESTORE HOPE, a humanitarian mission designed to reinforce the UN efforts and which would ultimately involve 25,000 U.S. service members.[50]

As RESTORE HOPE alleviated famine conditions, the newly-inaugurated Clinton administration expanded the short-term mission into a more expansive nation-building effort and it was this policy decision that triggered broader unintended consequences. Unbeknownst to American intelligence, Al-Qa'ida had a presence in Somalia and the HORN of Africa. In 1991 – 1992, bin Laden ordered extremists to Somalia to assist the Somali Islamic radical group *al-Ittihad al-Islamiya* (Islamic Unity) form an organized militia, in preparation to seize power of the war-torn country. As RESTORE HOPE was making the nightly news worldwide, bin Laden announced to those who were listening (Muslims in Arab states), that United States intervention in Somalia was an attempt at colonial occupation and a direct threat to Islam. Al-Qa'ida's first known terrorist attack against Americans occurred in the December 1992 bombing of a Yemeni hotel in Aden, used by American Soldiers traveling to Somalia to participate in RESTORE HOPE.[51] By early 1993, bin Laden issued a *fatwa* (religious edict) calling upon all Somalis to attack American forces and eject them from their country. He also dispatched several of his well trained cadre, including Mohammed Atef (planner for the 9/11 attacks), to train Somalis in military and terror tactics. The situation on the ground continued to worsen, and on June 5th, 1993 during a routine inspection of weapons storage facilities, U.N. peacekeepers were attacked by militia under the control of warlord Mohammed Farrah Aidid, resulting in twenty-five Pakistani soldiers killed and several wounded. Over the next four months, Aidid's followers would continue to conduct nightly mortar attacks into

UN compounds, random sniper attacks, assaults on compounds as well as small scale ambushes in order to constantly harass the peacekeeping efforts.[52]

On June 6, one day after the attack, the UN swiftly passed National Security Council Resolution (UNSCR) 837 (Somalia) condemning Aidid and his Somali National Alliance for the atrocity, and calling for the arrest and trial of those directly responsible.[53] The United States acted rapidly as well and under the auspices of UNSCR 837 formed a Joint Task Force under the United States Special Operations Command, to capture Aidid. Task Force Ranger, a joint force consisting of special operators from the Army, Navy, and Air Force special operations communities, deployed in August 2003 to Mogadishu airfield. But it was the battle on 3 October, during OPERATION GOTHIC SERPENT (raid to capture Aidid at the Olympia hotel), that Al-Qa'ida would catapult itself to the forefront of terror.[54] For it was over a 48-hour period that Al-Qa'ida trained Somalis would shoot-down U.S. Special Operations helicopters using a perfected technique of the Soviet-Afghan War (air burst modified RPGs), killing nineteen American warriors and wounding another 73, causing U.S. policy makers to quickly abandon the mission and order the immediate redeployment of forces.

The strategic effects of the Battle of Mogadishu ultimately set the tone for future foreign policy decisions by the Clinton administration. President Clinton would remain very reluctant to use military landpower for three future trouble spots (Rwandan Civil War between the Tutsis and Hutus, Bosnian War, and Kosovo War), due to an overwhelming fear of losing American Soldiers in combat and not wanting to suffer a repeat of Somalia. Another direct outcome of the policy decision made by President Clinton to withdraw at the first sign of casualties was not lost on Al-Qa'ida leaders.

Osama bin Laden and other radical Islamists would draw the conclusion that the way to drive to United States out of the Middle East, was to kill American Soldiers and use the media to achieve a greater psychological effect and influence the willpower of the American people. The perceived victory against the United States hyper-power in Somalia served as a catalyst to further inspire radical Islamist groups as well as increase anti-American sentiment amongst Islamic activists.

In the 1990s and on the heels of the Somalia conflict, Al-Qa'ida increased its activities to include deploying numerous Arab fighters to Bosnia to fight alongside their Muslim brothers.[55] Arab-Afghan *mujahidin* commanders arrived in Bosnia under the leadership of *Shaykh* Anwar Shaaban and *Amir* Abu Abdel Aziz Barbaros. Using the Afghan war model, commanders built camps and aggressively recruited and focused on training in both military tactics and fundamentalist ideology.[56] It was during the *Jihad* in Bosnia that Islamic charities and non-governmental organizations (NGOs) served a greater purpose, by funneling unaccounted for funding to support *Jihadi* organizations. The roots of the modern Al-Qa'ida financial network grew out of the Bosnian conflict as wealthy Arab organizations provided significant funding and terror financing networks appeared and grew roots.[57] Not only did the Arab *mujahidin* begin to win battles against Serb forces, but with the partnership of Muslim (Bosniak) and Croat forces and threat of NATO airpower, a favorable outcome was finally achieved. Even as the frontline against Serbian forces was closed upon the signing of the Dayton Peace Accords, a new generation of battle-tested *mujahidin* with the seeds of hatred and violence was being unleashed. The implementation of the Dayton Accords caused the Arab *mujahidin* to either go underground or exodus the Balkans, with many heading back to Afghanistan.

It was also during this time in the late 1990s, that terror attacks worldwide were increasing monumentally, as new terror cells continued to emerge and grow quietly across Europe and the Middle East. It was not until late 2000, when President Clinton was briefed on the failed millennium terrorist plot that the West truly understood the extensiveness of the underground Bosniak – Arab terrorist network.[58] The Bosnian War resulted in several significant advantages for Al-Qa'ida. The first was that recruits could train and hide from foreign law enforcement. Second, detailed planning for future operations could occur outside of the targeted countries and finally, Al-Qa'ida was one step closer towards infiltrating and establishing terror networks throughout Western Europe. The war also provided the ultimate meeting ground for North African Islamic cells, Saudi, Egyptian, Algerian, and Yemeni foreign fighter-leaders, greatly enhancing and advancing the Al-Qa'ida terror network. Bosnia would also serve as a historical battle cry and motivation for young Muslim recruits for future wars to include the current *Jihad* against the United States. For it was on the heels of the Bosnia War that bin Laden issued his next *fatwa,* openly declaring war against the United States.

Bin Laden's 1996 *fatwa* was first published in Al Quds Al Arabi, a London newspaper, in August 1996, titled the "Declaration of War against the Americans Occupying the Land of the Two Holy Places."[59] On the heels of the June 25, 1996 bombing of Khobar towers, located in Khobar, Saudi Arabia, the *fatwa* was a clear declaration of Al-Qa'ida interests and objectives and condemnation of U.S. military presence in Saudi Arabia. The lengthy discourse described an Islam under siege, and portrayed Muslims on the defensive, with no other option but to defend their religion through a call-to-arms and by violence.

On February 23, 1998, Al-Qa'ida issued its next *fatwa* signed by bin Laden and al-Zawahiri, *emir* of the *Jihad* group in Egypt, and cosigned by three other prominent Islamist leaders: Sheikh Mir Hamza, secretary of the *Jamiat-ul-Ulema-e-Pakistan*; Abu Yasir Rifa'l Ahmad Taha, head of the Egyptian Islamic Group; and Fazlur Rahman, *emir* of the Jihad movement in Bangladesh.[60] Although the basic message was consistent with that of the previous *fatwa*, it summarily stated:

> Under the banner of the "World Islamic Front for Combat Against Jews and Crusaders" (*al-Jabbah al-Islamiyya al-'Alamiyya li-Qital al-Yahud wal-Salibiyyin*) declaring the ruling to kill Americans and their allies both civilian and military, is the individual duty for every Muslim who can fight in any country in order for their armies to move out of the lands of Islam and to liberate the al-Aqsa Mosque (in Jerusalem) and the holy mosque (in Makka) from their grip. This being in the words of almighty Allah.[61]

Just six months later on August 7, Al-Qa'ida would strike again killing hundreds of civilians in near simultaneous car-bomb explosions outside the United States embassies in the African capital cities of Dar es Salaam, Tanzania, and Nairobi, Kenya. The attacks were conducted by local members of the growing greater Al-Qa'ida network of terrorist organizations. It was only African embassy attacks that the United States finally recognized the Al-Qa'ida as a viable and extremely capable adversary.[62] The United States responded to the attacks with cruise missile attacks deep into Afghanistan, near Khost, but failed to destroy or impede the Taliban and Al-Qa'ida training camps nor achieve the desired effective of deterring future terrorist attacks against the United States.

Based on the administrations limited military response and failed United States foreign policy in Somalia and Vietnam, bin Laden summarily detected a monumental vulnerability in the United States. He also understood that changes in U.S. policy in both the Vietnam and Somalia conflicts were due to the overwhelming influence of the willpower of the American people: ultimately the center of gravity of the United States. The significance of this insight is key; since historically terror targeted at intimidating and influencing a larger audience (people) would now become a mainstream of Al-Qa'ida's philosophy toward planning future targets and a key component within their overarching strategy against the United States.

In 2000, bin Laden turned his attention to Yemen, his ancestral homeland and plan for the next attack, against U.S. military power and Navy warships. On October 20, 2000, Al-Qa'ida aligned suicide martyrs would pilot a bomb-laden skiff into the *USS Cole*, a Navy Destroyer refueling in the port of Aden resulting in the death of seventeen sailors while another thirty-nine were wounded.[63] The success of this attack would further embolden and inspire Al-Qa'ida and other Islamist terrorist groups. Bin Laden and his followers rejoiced in Afghanistan at the success of the Cole attack and the silence that followed from the United States (no military response), was again perceived as weakness by America and its national leaders. Planning efforts for an even larger attack against the United States continued in earnest and in secret.

The attacks of 9/11 are well documented and, in one day, had an undisputable impact on the American psyche. America's sense of invulnerability and well-being was irreversibly shattered. Images of the World Trade Center crumbling upon itself will remain emblazoned in the minds of many, not only here in the homeland but also worldwide. For my generation, it was our day of infamy (much like the generation that experienced first hand the Japanese surprise attack on Peal Harbor, on December 7, 1941). For Al-Qa'ida it had manifested itself as the premier violent *Jihadist* movement, capable of global attack against the world's only remaining superpower (hyper-power).

They had ceased being a utopian group of *mujahidin* attempting to destroy existing political order, and had joined an exclusive club of apocalyptic terror groups where they were the sole member. What Al-Qa'ida failed to predict was the veracity of United States response and iron resolve in the wake of 9/11, and would soon find themselves and the Taliban bitterly embattled in Afghanistan and under fire. American forces fighting alongside Northern Alliance Afghan fighters would quickly route the Taliban and aligned Al Qa'ida fighters in Afghanistan and cause bin Laden and his core leadership cadre to take refuge in Pakistan, where they remain well-hidden today.

Present Day Al-Qa'ida and the Associated Movement (AQAM)

To better understand the present day Al-Qa'ida Associated Movement (AQAM), we must take the approach of analyzing the organization in "their own words and writings." Coalition forces fighting in Iraq and Afghanistan have uncovered an overabundance of documents authored by Al-Qa'ida members, which are stored and catalogued inside the Department of Defense "Harmony Project." Beginning in late 2005, the Combating Terrorism Center (CTC) at West Point was allowed access to numerous unclassified documents within the Harmony database and proceeded to study numerous Al-Qa'ida texts, *jihadi* images, video clips, statements, websites, as well as numerous other documents to include personal letters from AQAM senior leaders.[64] The Harmony Project, together with the proliferation of research over the past decade, has revealed much about the strategic objectives, ideology, and organizational structure of both Al-Qa'ida and the AQAM – the greater networked terror movement. By studying our enemy, through their own words, we can better understand them in order to effectively fight them.

Al-Qa'ida's Strategic Mission.

The strategic mission of Al-Qa'ida is through waging a *Jihad* (Holy War): 1) repulse Western influence (specifically the United States), out of Muslim states, especially the holy land (land of Mecca and Medina), 2) topple Arab and Muslim regimes that are corrupt and apostate (anti-Islamic) and, 3) install fundamentalist Islamic rule through a single Muslim nation (Caliphate) that would strictly govern in accordance with the *shari'a* (Islamic law). The strategic vision voiced by Osama Bin Laden and echoed by his Deputy Ayman al-Zawahiri is that Al-Qa'ida, or *"the base"*, will serve as the vanguard or *base* from which a greater worldwide global Jihad will be fought.[65]

1) Key Themes (Essential Tasks or General Goals).

- Spread *Jihad* throughout the Muslim nation.

- Prepare and train qualified Muslim personnel for *Jihad.*

- Support, aid, and help local *Jihadi* movements around the world.

- Coordinate international *Jihad* movements so as to create a united global *Jihad* movement.[66]

2) General Policies.

- Full adherence to the *shari'a* and the principles of all of our beliefs according to the *Qu'ran* and *Sunnah,* and the interpretations of the Al-Qa'ida scholars.

- To observe Jihad for the sake of God as a method of change and for each to strive for it and exercise it by all means necessary and available.

- To not have relations with world idols, the secular and national parties, or anything that resembles them. They are our enemies until at which time they believe in anything but God. We will not negotiate with them or agree to half-solutions.

- Our relations with the true *Jihadi* Islamic groups are based on cooperation, faith, and love of faith. We will continue in our efforts to unite and merge these groups and accept nothing less then cooperation and friendship.

- Relations with *non-Jihadi* Islamic groups will remain cordial; we acknowledge their good deeds but also tell them of their shortcomings if required.

- We will maintain complete independence and we will not follow any other party. We will maintain economic independence and not rely upon others for resources.

- With relations to our beloved Muslim scholars, we will show them love and respect and take only the good from them and advise them of what is incorrect.

- Secrecy is of utmost importance and is vital to our operations. We shall only reveal what we absolutely must reveal.

- Take an avid interest in the role of Muslim nations in *Jihad*, and attempt to not agitate them in order to gain support for *Jihad*. We reject regionalism and fanaticism. We are willing to perform *Jihad* anywhere within in the Muslim world if necessary.[67]

Al-Qa'ida The Organization.

We have learned much about Al-Qa'ida through the work of our intelligence agencies over the past seven years. The organization has proven exceptionally resilient and also extremely pragmatic when necessary. Al-Qa'ida has evolved from a centrally controlled and directed organization into a worldwide franchiser of terrorist groups and cells.[68] They have also selected a comparable lean business model for their internal organizational structure which is extremely secretive and shadowy. A basic understanding of roles and responsibilities of the core organization of Al-Qa'ida is important, so we can identify and exploit any weaknesses in the future. The core of Al-Qa'ida is best defined through the major components of the organization.

1) The *Emir* (The Commander). Osama bin Laden is the *Emir* (General or Commander) of Al-Qa'ida as well as the face of terror worldwide today. His duties are more in line with interpretation of spiritual guidance (he is not considered a theologian), strategic vision and direction, oversight of operational fronts, preeminent leader, and most respected member.[69] In many Muslim states, he is nearing almost mythical status, to some a visage of a modern day prophet who exudes influence through his inner circle of the trusted few, the *shura council*.

2) *Majlis al-shura council*. The role of the *shura* is to address issues of strategic importance, develop and recommend important policy that is consistent with the *Qu'ran* as well as interpretation of religious interpretations (for example the writings of Qutb), ensure guidance from the *emir* is followed, approve *fatwas*, and authorize major terrorist operations.[70] The most powerful entity within Al-Qa'ida, it is within this council that the strategic vision and directives are formulated and agreed upon. The Bylaws of the council are binding, as is the principle of *shura* (consultation) which is stipulated in the Qu'ran and was practiced by the Prophet Muhammad. Sessions are considered legal if and only when a quorum is reached, through regularly scheduled or emergency sessions and by preserving the principle of secrecy - often decided by secret ballots.[71] All *shura* members are handpicked by the *Emir* and all must have immeasurable experience with waging *jihad*, first hand, and in most cases many were with bin Laden during the early formulation of Al-Qa'ida in the 1980s. The council is purposely small and is comprised of the *Emir* (bin Laden), his Deputy (al-Zawahiri), a General Secretary

and averages between seven and ten total members.[72] The *shura* is as close as one can get to identify a center of gravity for Al-Qa'ida. The *shura* also oversees the work of the separate committees.

3) Al-Qa'ida Operational Committees. Al-Qa'ida has proven to be a patient well-organized and determined adversary. Six major committees (Military, Political, Information, Administration – Financial, Security, and Surveillance) serve to oversee the execution of day-to-day operations as well as other matters.

- Military Committee. Responsible for preparing young Islamic freedom fighters, training and organizing them for combat, and teaching them tactical and technical skills. Also develops and implements procedures for the greater fighting forces in accordance with Islamic law. The committee is subdivided into five separate divisions of the President, training-combat, training-operations, nuclear weapons section, and library and research section.[73] The general goals of the committee are to organize and supervise combat participation on the battlefield, recruitment and enlistment, upward development and mobility of *Jihadi* fighters, and ensuring Al-Qa'ida fighters are experts in resistance warfare.[74] The mere fact there exists a nuclear operations section is more evidence that Al-Qa'ida is fully determined to obtain and use weapons of mass destruction.

- Political Committee. Responsible for the spreading of political awareness amongst all members and between Al-Qa'ida and Islamic republics. Also this committee conducts research and political studies and is principally responsible for interaction between Al-Qa'ida and with other Jihadi organizations. The organizational structure consists of a president of the committee, a representative to the president, a political section, and operational political officers.[75] A common theme promulgated by the committee is the political goals of the Al-Qa'ida movement, and that the movement of *Jihad* is the reinforcement of God's solution and rightful path of Islam. The foundations of religious interpretation, married within the political context is the major work of this committee, with the ultimate goals of spreading awareness and inspiring collective efforts within the greater *Jihadi* movement. The work of this body is also a vulnerability, which I will address later in this paper.

     - Information Committee. A recognized significant strength for Al-Qa'ida, this committee is concerned with all matters with respect to the means of communications information in all categories of Islamic people. The goals of the committee are to:

          - Call upon all Muslims to embark on a *jihad*, as the true word of God, and in the name of Islam.

          - Spread and enforce the general rules and concepts of Al-Qa'ida ideology (includes *Salafism*, *Qutbism* and when necessary *takfir*).

          - Conduct information operations to spread the ideology and ignite global *Jihad*. Attack the West wherever and whenever possible and do so using informational jurisprudence in accordance with the *shari'a*.

          - Uncover, reveal, and exploit the weaknesses of secular governments and nationalist parties. Reinforce the importance of Islamic *Jihad* as each Muslim's individual mission.[76]

Responsible for the overall strategic communications of Al-Qa'ida, its leadership and targeted at both Islamic and non-Islamic audiences. The United States needs to address this Al-Qa'ida strength and our weaknesses in this area, in order to make headway and counter this Al-Qa'ida strength. At present, Al-Qa'ida has hijacked the message of Islam amongst the dearth of Islamic activists and is refashioning information to press its messages and further their strategic interests at the expense of the majority of moderate or non-violent Muslims.

- Administration and Financial Committee. This committee functions to undertake the different administrative services for Al-Qa'ida members and their families to include salaries, vacations and leave, disability and medical benefits, as well as severance benefits. In addition, they are responsible for all accounting to include safeguarding funding, as well as tracking payments and costs, provide loans if needed, while overseeing financial policies and services for the organization.[77]

- Security Committee. The committee responsible for providing the necessary operational security for the leadership, operations, installations, and personnel. It routinely collects information required for security as well as promoting personal feeling of security. It also facilitates security procedures related to any host country in accordance with bylaws, legal laws, and regulations. Within this committee security bylaws are crafted and implemented in order to preserve the integrity and capability of the greater organization. With respect to dangerous matters the committee looks at possible infiltration, corruption as well as vulnerabilities. Led by a committee chairman, the committee is comprised of a lesser council, and an executive branch which includes an investigations section, imprisonments and torture section, documents section, and coordination and relations section. The guard detail also falls within the purview of this committee as well as passports section and security education.[78]

Arguably, this vital committee has excelled at its duties due to the mere fact that the senior leadership of the *shura* council remains protected and safe, even after seven years of waging a war with the United States.

- Surveillance Committee. The details of this committee are classified as well as its full range of responsibilities and capabilities. However, we can assume that this functional arm of the inner organization has an extremely important role, specifically with regards to reconnaissance, surveillance and target recommendations for future large scale Al-Qai'da attacks.

What is important to understand is that although Al-Qa'ida "higher headquarters" closely mirrors other historical examples of insurgent organizations (most closely to Mao with the Chinese and the Vietcong), it is extremely adaptable and quickly learns from its vulnerabilities; therefore, to date, has been elastic enough to overcome any inefficiencies or vulnerabilities. The organization is also less rigid today within the context of the greater movement (AQAM). The *emir* openly seeks operational recommendations from field commanders, subordinates, and partnered *Jihadi* groups. It is the uniqueness of this form of command and control (decentralized) structure that makes normal Western center of gravity targeting methodology, ineffective at best. Al-Qa'ida has inspired and created the greater Al-Qa'ida Associated Movement (AQAM) consisting of a collective of Islamist *Jihadi* organizations (sans the *shura* and primary committees), into a loose global-network of interrelated ideological groups, who engage in *Jihad* and terror (a common theme) for either local, regional, or global objectives, of which Al-Qa'ida exploits to what is being perceived as a global insurgency or global holy war. It is through our understanding of the organizational structure, the mission and objectives of the organization, and its importance within a greater movement, of where we can begin to identify and then exploit vulnerabilities.

<u>Al-Qa'ida Strategy towards the United States and Emerging Jihadi Doctrine</u>.

Al Qa'ida strategy is not fueled solely by hatred nor are its desired ends, inconsistent with their methods and means to engage in protracted *Jihad*. But rather, their strategy is very consistent and nested within their ideology, and they make strategic decisions with detached methodical precision, constantly assessing alternative approaches as well as seeking additional means or methods. Analysts have uncovered several indicators that they believe Al-Qa'ida continues to prepare and plan for another large scale synchronized attack against the United States, while the AQAM will continue to plot and execute numerous smaller scale attacks, likely against soft targets in the near future which is more broadly in line with the general aim of punishing non-believers.[79]

Al-Qa'ida Grand Strategy.

Jordanian analyst Bassam al-Baddarin believes Al-Qa'ida has formulated a strategy out through 2020. Referencing the assorted writings of Muhammad Makkawi (better known as Sayf al-Adel, former Egyptian Special Forces Colonel and now one of al-Qaeda's senior strategists), Al-Adel presents a coherent long-term strategy that ties together the events of 9/11 and the current fronts on terror in Afghanistan and Iraq. Initially, the head of the Military training branch, al-Adel is believed to have surpassed Abu Hafs al-Masri as the new Al-Qa'ida #3 behind al-Zawahiri, bin Laden's Deputy. Al-Adel's writings indicate a strategic campaign formulated against America, aimed at leveraging a *jihadist* "triangle of terror" beginning in Afghanistan, passing through Iran and Iraq, and ending in Southern Turkey. The 9/11 attack, commenced the opening phase of war against America, intended to drag the United States into Islamic lands to enable Al-Qa'ida to wage a long war of attrition against the West utilizing the awakening giant of the greater Islamic nation.[80] Baddarin hypothesizes that Al-Qa'ida knowingly intentionally abandoned the Taliban and transferred a significant part of its Arab fighting strength to Iran and Iraq, expecting a swift response into Afghanistan by U.S. Military forces. He argues that Al-Qa'ida predicted the United States response against the Taliban regime in Afghanistan (both host and bed partners with Al-Qa'ida), and would then pursue a more comprehensive military effort against Iraq.[81] Adding credibility to this theory is the importance of Abu Musab al-Zarqawi leaving Afghanistan in 2002, and establishing a base of operations in Northern Iraq, well before the Coalition invasion of Iraq in March of 2003.

An additional published work available on the internet for all *Jihadists* with significant insights to a greater Al-Qa'ida grand strategy in the Middle East, is Abu Bakir Naji's "Management of Savagery." Published by the Center of Islamic Studies and Research (an Al-Qa'ida affiliated entity), Naji's work outlines the progressive stages of establishing a true Islamic state. Naji is a well respected *Jihadi* author as many of his writings are published on the *Sawt al-Jihad* online website as well as his background and experience in *Jihad*.[82] The Olin Institute for Strategic Studies at Harvard University in partnership with the West Point CTC, commissioned William McCants to translate this important strategic text. A "Path towards empowerment" is an underlying theme that serves to unite all *Jihadi* organizations and *mujahidin* and Naji embeds numerous quotes from *Qu'ranic* text, to further his arguments and strategy. What follows is the genesis of Naji's grand strategy for *Jihad* in the Middle East. [83]

Naji identifies three distinct phases with goals:

- The Destruction and Exhaustion Phase. The *mujahidin* will exhaust the United States by over commitment, and exhaustion as well as attract new recruits by exploiting successful attacks such as the bombings in Bali (nightclub bombing claiming 200 lives),[84] Al-Muhayya (residential compound in Saudi Arabia – 2003),[85] and the attack on the Djerba (synagogue in Tunis – 2002).[86]

- The Management of Barbarism-Savagery Phase. After defeating Western forces, the *mujahidin* will establish internal security, ensure the people have the necessary food and supplies, medical access and support, economic sufficiency is achieved and infrastructure improvements have begun. It is also during this phase that implementation of *shari'a* justice begins; fighters are prepared for external attacks as well as defending against internal hypocrisy and deviant opinions in order to enforce strict obedience. Alliances will be made with neighbors who have yet to conform.[87]

- The Empowerment Phase. This phase features a continuation of the major objectives of the previous phase while at the same time establish logistic links with the various zones outside the immediate zone of conflict. An important objective to achieve in this phase is the development and execution of a powerful media and information campaign in order to win support and increase recruitment, as well as push others in the middle ranks to join in *Jihad*.[88]

Numerous other writings and messages are available by researching the many *Jihadi* websites across the Internet. What is significant to the United States counterterrorism effort is that Al-Qa'ida is not hiding their strategy, their objectives, or their desire to create a wider global effect of interlinked terror groups conducting terror campaigns. Further analysis of this literature reveals that the emerging strategy against America is aimed at our centers of gravity, our economy, and our willpower.

Al-Qa'ida Strategy with respect to the United States

The operational strategy for neutralizing the United States combines both passive and active activities. Al Qa'ida strategists have studied and clearly understand the vital interests of the United States, and are developing a comprehensive strategy to attack our two centers of gravity: 1) our economic well-being/survival and 2) American willpower or the staying power to endure a protracted war against terror. To accomplish these foals Al-Qa'ida will continue to orchestrate and order direct attacks against the United States homeland, its citizens at home and abroad, its military, and its economic interests. In addition, they intend to ensure the Muslim world is inhospitable for United States business interests as well as for political engagement with Islamic leaders.[89]

Bin Laden and Al-Qa'ida fully intend to wage war against what they perceive as our primary vulnerabilities. Bin Laden claims that since the abolition of the Caliphate in 1924, Western Crusades have worked to prevent the true believers (Muslims) from establishing an Islamic state. Much of his rhetoric also labels the United States as most responsible for the ocean of repression, injustices toward Muslims, and that the Al-Qa'ida attacks of 9/11 were warranted and just.[90] The attacks against iconic American targets on 9/11 were clearly intended to cripple the economic, political, and military power of the United States as well as severely hamper our ability to respond. The emblematic importance of the World Trade Center, the Pentagon, and the object of the third attack (White House, Congress or the Three Mile Island Power Plant) was essential for Al Qa'ida and their desire to achieve a greater psychological impact than on those persons directly affected in both New York and Washington. The attack in New York alone not only impacted the American economy, but many experts believe severely affected the world economy to the tune of trillions of dollars in losses.[91] The financial backlash of the 9/11 attacks were momentous (mostly felt in tourism, financial markets, and the airline industry), debatably contributed to a national recession.[92] Al-Qa'ida leaders learned many important lessons from the 9/11 attacks and will likely continue with a terror campaign to focus on soft targets that greatly impact the American people both economically and by attempting to make this a long, endless struggle and violent clash of civilizations that cannot be won.

In October 2005, Abu Mus'ab al-Najadi, a Saudi and active member of Al-Qa'ida authored a document entitled, "Al-Qaida's Battle is Economic not Military." He argued for attacking soft targets of high economic interests. al-Najadi's words are very telling:

> The Islamic nation has entered through Al-Qaid's war with America a new period that is different from all other periods experienced by Muslims against their enemies. This period is based on economic war due to the peculiar nature of the adversary in this ferocious battle. Usually wars are based on military strength and victory belongs to those who are militarily superiors on the battlefield... But our war with America is fundamentally different for the first priority is defeating her economically...[93]

What we are likely to experience in the future is attacks on targets that will have both a huge psychological impact upon Americans, as well as a corresponding economic ripple. Terror attacks on our subways, railways, and the airline industry will certainly create hysteria, panic, and incite fear, while costing the United States millions of dollars. Attacks within the Middle East against oil infrastructure or shipping would wreck havoc in world markets as well as cause skyrocketing crude oil prices, further

41

causing economic backlash as global markets scramble to absorb these blows. The methods of attacks are also important to understand, for it is clearly evident that Al-Qa'ida has adopted and is following a doctrine of 4th-generation warfare.

Al-Qa'ida Emerging Doctrine and 4th-Generation Warfare.

Al-Qa'ida associated terror cells have shown a mastery of operational ingenuity in their selection of hard and soft targets (political, military, economic, iconic, and religious). Through their application of the fundamentals of 4th-generation warfare (4GW), they have continued to achieve small tactical victories and avoid defeat at the hands of Coalition forces in a complex and austere environment. 4GW is the evolution of warfare over time, starting with the 1st-generation (Napoleonic warfare – conscription and firepower) through the 2nd-generation (U.S. Civil War/World War I – age of firepower and nation-state aligned resources), through the 3rd-generation (World War II – maneuver and armored warfare) and up to a 4th-generation near the end of the 20th century. 4GW is considered the reduction of nation-state warfare and is fought primarily by ad-hoc warrior cells which have embraced the following concepts:

- Undermine your enemy's strength (avoid direct attacks or attacks on operational/tactical centers of gravity – aka von Clausewitzian doctrine).

- Exploit your enemy's weaknesses and vulnerabilities.

- Fight utilizing asymmetric operations (weapons and tactics will differ substantially from those of your enemy).[94]

The methods of 4GW warfare are unmistakably apparent on the front lines of the war on terror in both Iraq and Afghanistan. Improvised Explosive Devices (IEDs) as well as suicide bombers (martyrdom) are two prominent methods used by radical insurgents, to counter Coalition strengths such as overwhelming firepower and a maneuver based doctrine. Both of these tactics are relatively low cost, easy to execute, with a high payoff and have a greater psychological effect on both military forces as well as Americans at home. Americans that are being greatly influenced through watching horrific images of the aftereffects of an IED attack on their televisions in the comfort of their homes. 4GW is intended to exhaust one's opponent and cause him to use up his resources through slow attrition, while fighting over a protracted length of time. We may, in fact, be witness to a 5th-generation of warfare (5GW) that emerges in this century, and is one where advances in technology, to include the new media and explosion in information warfare, and proliferation of weapons of mass effects in the hands of transnational or non-state actors, becomes the norm.

Further evidence that Al-Qa'ida has adopted a form of 4GW as its primary doctrine of modern warfare can be found in the writings of *Jihadi* ideologue, Abu Musab al-Suri (aka Mustafa Setmariam Nasar). Posted on *Jihadi* websites, his January 2005 work titled "The Global Islamic Resistance Call" provides a strategic template for global *Salafi-Jihad*.[95] Through his writings, and from his first hand experience from Afghanistan, the primary tenants of Al-Suri's adaptation of 4GW lie within the philosophy of *nizam la tanzim* (system not organization). This phrase mirrors a number of tenants of 4GW and demonstrates a clear understanding of decentralized operations, commander's intent, and dispersal of leadership and *mujahidin* fighters across countless battlefields. Al-Suri believes that his model for warfare and adaptation of Western 4GW doctrine will allow for the implementation of a self-sustaining global insurgency.[96] The current trend we are witnessing today is one of a decreasing reliance of terror cells worldwide on operational guidance and logistical support from the core Al-Qa'ida leadership.

The strategy of Martyrdom tactics (Suicide bombers).

Suicide terrorism has had a long and unequivocal role in politics and conflict throughout history. Suicide tactics are not new to modern warfare. In 19th century Japan, *Inin-Shishi Ronins* led by Miyabe Teizo, conducted close quarters battle suicide attacks against legitimate forces and authorities of the Shogun,[97] while the early 20th century Muslim Malays (*Moros*) were known for their favored chaotic suicidal tactics to include frantic knife fighting close combat with American Soldiers in the Philippines.[98]

Japanese Kamikaze pilots in World War Two are one of the more prominent cases of suicide tactics in warfare; however, unlike Islamist terror groups who sponsor and encourage suicide attacks, the Kamikazes exclusively attacked legitimate military targets, as opposed to noncombatants. During the last stages of war with Japan, suicide pilots were enlisted as a strategic weapon to incite fear amongst the American Navy and achieve a larger psychological effect in American willpower and national leaders. Air attacks against the U.S. Navy managed to sink thirty-four ships and damage an additional 368, while killing an estimated 3,900 sailors; all at the cost of 2,800 suicide pilots.[99] Al-Qa'ida inspired suicide bombers (Islamist martyrs) in Iraq have focused an estimated ninety percent of their attacks against Iraqi civilians and security personal (the other ten percent were against Coalition forces). An estimated 2006 United States service members have been killed as a result of these suicide attacks since 2003, while Iraqi estimates of civilian deaths are well over 10,000.[100] Although both the Kamikazes and Islamic martyrs goal was to create a psychological effect of fear amongst a larger audience ultimately in hopes of a change in policy and force an end to the conflict (U.S. ceasing attacks against Japan or U.S. retreating from Iraq in order to then openly incite a civil sectarian war), each targeted different groups to achieve that effect, yet both failed in achieving their objectives.

Al-Qa'ida espouses the tactic of suicide bombers (martyrdom) as a fundamental element of their strategy of terror for the following reasons: 1) symbology of the attack method (bomber is a martyr in the context of a religious *Jihad-Holy War*, one that is justified by *Qu'ranic* interpretation), 2) the ultimate "smart" bomb that is inexpensive and efficient, 3) enhances the image of both the organization and the individual bomber (the reward of heaven and entitlements afforded to martyrs), 4) nearly impossible to stop or defend against, and 5) effective in that an attack almost always reaches a larger audience and achieves larger effects. Al-Qa'ida inspired *Jihadis* have expertly exploited the religious, social, cultural, and political symbols of martyrdom in order to appeal to a wider Muslim audience, beyond the core of Al-Qa'ida loyalists.

Yoram Schweitzer, a former Israeli intelligence officer and now a researcher at the Jaffee Research Center for Strategic Studies (JCSS), Tel Aviv University, conducted ninety-seven formal interviews of Palestinian suicide terrorists captured by the Israelis. Of the eighty males and seventeen females he interviewed (thirty-one were actual bombers, the others were cell members of suicide attack cells), he concluded that every operation was executed in order to achieve political effects to weaken the legitimacy of the group's adversary; the government (Israel or the United States – the mightiest of adversaries).[101] Al-Qa'ida has adopted the suicide attacks as a key component of their overarching strategy and this is most evident by their ongoing campaign in Iraq against the *Shi'as*.

Dr. Mohammed M. Hafez, in his book <u>Suicide Bombers in Iraq: The Strategy and Ideology of Martyrdom</u> thoroughly analyzes the ongoing suicide phenomena and Al-Qa'ida suicide campaign in Iraq against the broader international implications for the future. Dr. Hafez's most prolific observations are:

- Although suicide attacks did not exist in Iraq before the U.S. occupation, correlation is not causation of the ongoing phenomena.[102]

- While previous suicide attacks by Palestinian groups (for example the Lebanese Hizbullah attack on the U.S. Marines and French forces in 1983, Lebanon) were a component of a strategy for liberation against democracies with forces who posed an imminent threat to control territory that the terrorists viewed as their homeland, *Salafi-Jihadi* terrorism is intended to incite a secular civil war in Iraq.[103] A civil war that the U.S would find untenable and subsequently withdraw, allowing Al-Qa'ida to establish a base for future *Jihad* in the region as well as move forward along the path toward a true Islamic state or caliphate.

- Psychological trauma is likely one root cause of volunteers of suicide attacks, but is not the motivation of why *Salafi-Jihadi* organizations opt to plan, coordinate, and conduct suicide terror attacks.

- The majority of suicide attacks in Iraq are aimed at defenseless *Shia* noncombatants. The *Shi'a* response to the indiscriminate bombing campaign was conducted by the Sadr (Muqtada al-Sadr) militia, specifically covert death squads which engaged in abductions, torture, and extrajudicial murder against everyday *Sunnis*.[104]

- Al-Qa'ida or *Sunni* groups that promote suicide attacks have used writings, ritual, and ceremony to foster a cult like status for martyrs. Fanaticism is deeply rooted in the Saudi *Wahhabi* doctrine and *takfir* extremism. The preponderance of *Sunni* suicide bombers are not Iraqis by birth, but have volunteered as martyrs to wage in *Jihad* and come from outside Iraq.[105]

- Former *emir* of Al-Qa'ida in Iraq (AQIZ), Abu Musab al-Zarqawi's logic to promote suicide tactics in Iraq was a deep desire to spark sectarian violence, in order to drag the hesitant *Sunni* population into the conflict. Upon achieving this, he could then establish the conditions for foreign *Jihadis* to operate freely and amongst the host *Sunni* populace.[106]

Martyrdom attacks continued to flourish and transnational martyrs flocked to Iraq, largely due to the major shocks to the country in a relatively short period of time. Rapid regime change, collapse of the entire security apparatus and rule of law, growing disenfranchisement of the populace, ineffective government and deterioration of the security situation over time, resentment and fear amongst a sectarian populace (*Kurds, Shi'as and Sunnis*) provided fertile ground for Al-Qa'ida to grow roots and thrive amongst the *Sunnis*. But the answer to the question of why are suicide attacks a central component to current Al-Qa'ida strategy, is best comprehended by understanding the pragmatism of Al-Qa'ida leaders and the adaptability and evolution of the organization.

Dr. Hafez argues that 1st-generation *Jihadis* of the Soviet-Afghan War did not adopt suicide terrorism as a key component to their overall strategy. But, the current generation (2nd-generation) clearly understood the success of the Palestinians acceptance of the tactic during conflicts in Lebanon and Palestine. Martyrs were afforded special recognition and legitimacy mainly due to the fact religious scholars argued that these acts were a legitimate form of *Jihad* and devotion to the Islamic faith.[107] Muslims have come to support the tactic from the ideological stance that these methods are legitimate through *Qu'ranic* interpretation and they are legitimate weapons against regimes or powers with more capable military forces and technological superiority. In straightforward terms, the *Jihadi* "smart weapon" a low cost, highly accurate and high payoff weapon of choice. It is extremely likely that the next or next generation of *Jihadis* will expand suicide terrorism to include a weapon of mass effects - destruction. Al-Qa'ida has the motivation, desire and aspirations to achieve apocalyptic transnational terror status and will continue to pursue the capability unless they are stopped or destroyed.

The strategy of waging asymmetric warfare through suicide attacks is a clear strength for Al-Qa'ida and the *Salafi-Jihadi* terrorist groups. It is also a significant vulnerability in that its legitimacy with regards to Islamic jurisprudence can be directly challenged.

Al Qa'ida Strengths, Weaknesses - Vulnerabilities.

With a solid comprehension of who our enemy is (Al-Qa'ida), their organizational structure, strategy, and doctrine, we can now identify and address the strengths and vulnerabilities of our transnational foe.

1) Strengths. Al-Qa'ida has numerous strengths but the following six are indispensable to their organization and their greater stimulated movement.

a) Decentralized Execution – Hidden Terror Cells. As previously stated, the structure and organization is one that is less a hierarchical command and control apparatus, but one of senior leadership providing strategic guidance, general direction, and intent for the greater movement. *Jihadis* and terrorist cells are slowly multiplying and spreading worldwide like cancer and, because of their exceptional operational security methods, it is extremely difficult for counterterrorist forces to identify, track, and kill/capture these elements. The AQAM is a loosely connected network of terror groups and cells that share common ideological goals and the universally agreed method of achieving their political ends – through violence.

b) <u>Ideology and Doctrine: Nested within the *Qu'ran* and Islam</u>. Al-Qa'ida ideology is one that has evolved over time and is a by-product of three prominent undercurrents within *Sunni* theology. Al-Qa'ida's loyal *Jihadis* consist of radical activists whose unswerving commitment to violence is part of a larger struggle to defend *Dar al-Islam* (House of Islam – the area of the world historically subject to Muslim rule), and the defense of the *umma*, against infidel enemies.[108] The three currents most present in AQAM terror groups are as follows:

- The *Salafiyya al-jihadiyya* (*Salafi Jihadis*), composed of radicalized Muslims who believe in the Egyptian strand of *Sunni Salafi* ideology and who embrace violence and wage in the *Jihad*.

- The *al Qutbiyyan* (*Qutbists*), composed of extremist Muslims who believe in the ideology born of Egyptian Sayyid Qutb, and who focus on the nearer enemy, or local apostate regimes such as Egypt and Saudi Arabia, before fighting a "*Global Jihad*" against the far enemy (Israel and the West).

- *Hizb ut-Takfir al-Islami* (*Takfir*) or those extremists who openly practiced the calling of unbelievers or Muslims who have abandoned Islam, as a *kafir*.[109]

Al-Qa'ida strategy and doctrine is built upon the foundations of all major schools of *Sunni* teachings with a heavy reliance on militant *Salafism*. The *Salafis* are opposed to both *Shi'a* and *Sufi* doctrines and reject Western ideologies such as Socialism and Capitalism, political parties, and social justice. As described earlier, the *Jihadis* come from the constituency of the *Salafists* who are a subset of the greater group of Islamists. *Jihadis* draw upon the noted scholars and theologians of each sect in order to craft their ideology and subsequently their operational doctrines. Speeches, *fatwas*, and web postings by senior Al-Qa'ida leaders and operational field commanders always include quotes from the *Qu'ran*, further adding legitimacy to their words since every Muslim respects the writings of the *Qu'ran* as the irrefutable words of God. The operational doctrine formulated and then followed by Al-Qa'ida is firmly entrenched within their ideology, and this is easily the greatest strength of the movement.

Ideology also plays the pivotal role in recruitment for Al-Qa'ida. Driven by their particular vision for the future, Al-Qa'ida uses images, Islamic text, videos, et cetera, in order to appeal to potential recruits as well as for support from a great Islamic audience.[110] Universities, mosques, and the worldwide network of *madrassas* and *pesantren* (Muslim boarding schools), are the fertile grounds in which the extremist ideology is being planted, with the goal of growing future terrorists and supporters of their greater cause.[111]

c) <u>Opportunists and Pragmatists - Catalyst within Islam</u>. Islam has long been a religion of conflict and the Middle East has been a region that has borne witness to near-constant conflict since well before the Roman Legions arrived in the first century

AD. The current struggle within Islam today is one of either accepting modernity into society or rejecting it, for fear of it surpassing the role of religion.[112]

Quinton Wiktoriwicz, in his work Islamic Activisim: A Social Movement Theory Approach, proposes that by utilizing a social movement theory approach as a guiding framework for researchers, we can better analyze the ongoing trend of Islamist activism. He contends that the process, dynamics, and organizations of Islamic activists can be better understood as critical elements in contention with one another that transcend Islam.[113] Islamic activism, the mobilization of support for Muslim causes, is undoubtedly the greater ongoing phenomena that Al-Qa'ida is leveraging to increase its appeal and support base. One important consistent factor Wiktoriwicz and a collective of Islamic activism social movement theorists observed, is that current Islamic activists are blaming the West and Western values for a wide variety of societal problems, such as rising unemployment, increasing debt, inadequate or insufficient housing, and stagnant economic growth, et cetera.[114] The effects of globalization has also given rise to Islamist activism.

Globalization and the advancement of communication technologies that came with it have afforded Islamist activists a greater voice in the Middle East as well as across the Islamic nation. But the West continues to muddy the waters by misidentifying and stereotyping Islamic activists with *Jihadis* or fundamentalists.

Islamism is synonymous with "Islamist activism or Political Islam," the act of asserting and promoting beliefs, norms, laws, and policies that are held to be Islamic in character.[115]

Western dialogue tends to identify "Islamic activism" as a singular phenomenon, and erroneously label it Islamism or "Political Islam" or worse "Islamic Fundamentalism."

The term, Political Islam is a Western idiom which came into our lexicon about the time of the Iranian Revolution. It is critical to grasp that Islam is not only a religion, or a religion of peace, but it is also a religion of law, therefore, it is inherently concerned with both governance and politics.[116] Islam permeates everything to include politics, economics, as well as social and legal systems.

By mistakenly juxtaposing all Islamists into one single group, we are overlooking essential factors that differentiate how Islamists outwardly express their convictions. Islamists can range from militants or fundamentalists to moderates, and everything in between that wide-ranging continuum. Al-Qa'ida exemplifies the militant extreme and fundamentalist spectrum of Islamist activism.

Al-Qa'ida views itself as the vanguard of change and is serving as the catalyst by drawing the United States into a greater Islamic Insurgency through the attacks of 9/11. Incredulously, a large segment of Islamists are considered "moderates," thus the extremists are the minority. Moderates can be recognized by two separate attitudes: 1) those who believe that a peaceful path to change exists and is achievable or 2) those that believe Islam can reform and reconcile itself with Western modernity. Save for the current problem in that Al-Qa'ida and the radical extremists have uniformly hijacked all Islamic dialogue and the voice of the moderates is drowned out and cannot be heard over the violent sandstorms of radical rhetoric.

Osama bin Laden and his deputy, Ayman al-Zawahiri, are not only militant radical *Jihadis* inspired by *Salafi* and *Qutb* ideological writings, they are also extremely pragmatic in their strategy towards a global *Jihad*. Bin Laden's pragmatic and adaptive leadership methods are evident through his loose management style and infrequent communiqués to the growing coalition of *Jihadi* organizations. He has implemented very few regulations and non-negotiable rules, but sternly demands compliance.

The relationship with the now deceased Abu Musab al-Zarqawi, a true *takfir* radical extremist, was built on a marriage of convenience in order to inspire additional recruits, as well as to continue to tie-down and exhaust American military power in irregular warfare in Iraq. What bin Laden and Al-Qa'ida central did not expect nor approve was the beginnings of a sectarian civil war in Iraq, that was ignited by the February 2006 bombing of the *Shi'a* Al-Askari Mosque "Golden Dome Mosque," Samarra, Iraq. Considered worldwide as one of the holiest *Shi'a* shrines, Al-Qa'ida in Iraq (AQIZ) *Jihadis* planned and executed attacks that would incite a civil war in Baghdad between the *Sunnis* and *Shi'a* militias.[117]

Today, Al-Qa'ida senior leaders appear to be continuing along pragmatic lines as there is increasing evidence that Al-Qa'ida is reaching across ideological lines to establish relationships with *Shi'a* terror groups such as Hamas, as well as entering into a strategic relationship of convenience with Iranian leaders (Persian *Shi'as*).[118] Hamas and Al-Qa'ida are both modern offshoots of the original *Jihadi* organization, the Muslim Brotherhood, and share many links dating back to pre - 9/11 attacks.[119] Al-Qa'ida and Hamas have a history together, but an Iran and Al-Qa'ida connection could further be exploited if exposed, and would negatively impact Al-Qa'ida credibility based on their *Salafi* and *Qutbist* ideological underpinnings.

      d) <u>No Center of Gravity (A Counter to U.S. Warfighting Doctrine)</u>. In the past three decades, the warfighting concept of center(s) of gravity has become an integral part of our Joint and Service doctrines. Identifying enemy center(s) of gravity and protecting our own has become a cornerstone of the operational art of our maneuver and firepower based doctrine. The origins of center of gravity were forwarded by the notable Prussian military theorist, Carl von Clausewitz in his seminal work, <u>On War</u>.[120] However, there exists a minority of professional military thinkers to include this author, who believe von Clausewitz's original intent of center of gravity has been misconstrued by U.S. military doctrine writers and senior leadership. Antulio Echevarria, an United States Army officer argued in his 2002 published work <u>Clausewitz's Center of Gravity: Changing Our Warfighting Doctrine – Again</u>!, that Clausewitz's concept of center of gravity (CoG) was not intended as a strength or a weakness, nor even a source of strength, but that the CoG was the **one** element within a combatant's entire structure or system that has the necessary centripetal force to bind and truss the entire system together.[121] This happening is what Clausewitz theorized when powerful strikes oriented against this CoG would have the most significant effect, as opposed to solely a mechanical or scientific explanation of force against an enemy's CoG that would ensure success. Echevarria argues that Clausewitz intended the CoG not as a basis of strength or a key function or capability, but more a central point that is essentially effects-based, as opposed to capabilities based. Attacking an adversary's center of gravity through mass and with overwhelming force will cause your enemy to lose his balance and then eventually topple and fall. A center of gravity according to Clausewitz is not a source of strength, but more a factor of balance. [122]

To date our strategic and operational strategies have been focused on identifying and attacking the center of gravity(s) of Al-Qa'ida, which has resulted in minimal tactical gains. The Al-Qa'ida core leadership and funding for Islamist terrorist organizations have been misidentified as the source of their strength, or center(s) of gravity. These are certainly strengths and must be both targeted and influenced, but the source of balance or centripetal force binding Al-Qa'ida together is something less visible or concrete, and much harder to comprehend and counter. The force in question is their ideology which infuses a common hatred of apostate Muslim regimes and anti-Americanism sentiment both amongst its core members and supporters, and throughout the larger Islamic audience.

e) Information Operations and Strategic Communications. Al-Qa'ida is exceptionally adept at communicating and influencing larger target audiences with their themes and messages. Our government officials agree that our efforts at public diplomacy continue to be outmaneuvered by our foe. Al-Qa'ida is extremely adept at influencing the *Jihadis* within their organization and the supporters of *Jihadi* cells, local population areas, the Arab community, the greater Islamic community and, in general the world population. The rapid expansion and significant improvements in communications technology that have been the major drivers of globalization have benefited Al-Qa'ida in its efforts to build and maintain trust and credibility with Muslims. Clearly, their messages are multiplied and exponentially reproduced across the entire media spectrum and especially the Internet.

Gabriel Weimann, Senior Fellow at the United States Institute of Peace (USIP), provides an interesting glimpse into how terrorist organizations are using the Internet.

In his book, <u>Terror on the Internet: The New Arena, The New Challenges</u>, Weimann highlights the advantages that the World Wide Web affords terrorist groups and the challenges of and options available to countering terrorist use of the Internet.[123] A summary of his observations are:

- The Internet affords *Jihadis* ease of access, little or no regulation – government control or censorship, large potential global audiences, limitless – fast information flow through a multi-media format, and anonymity.

- All active terrorist groups are established on the Internet (hundreds to thousands of web sites and increasing daily).

- Dynamic interaction on the web: sites emerge, modify, then abruptly disappear – or appear to disappear but only change the *url* address to enhance security and communications.

- Three distinct target audiences have been identified: current or potential supporters, international public opinion, adversary public (opinions and political will).

- Over exaggeration of the cyber-terrorism threat (impending cyber attacks), at the expense of the more common routine use of terrorist communications and strategic communications – information operations.

- Eight most common methods in which terror groups use the internet (psychological warfare, publicity and propaganda, fundraising, recruitment and mobilization, data mining, networking, information sharing, and planning and coordination.

- Future measures to cyber-terrorism and internet usage by terrorist entities, will not only be costly and difficult, but will inevitability flirt dangerously with civil liberties and freedom of speech.[124]

An irrefutable strength of modern-day terrorist organizations and Al-Qa'ida is their focus on multiple target audiences with specific messages for each to influence and co-opt them, and that the themes and subsequent messages are embedded within their unique interpretations of the *Qu'ran* and the *Sunnah* (interpretation through the living example of the Prophet Muhammed).[125] The United States has little to no credibility in the Muslim world and Al-Qa'ida has seized this opportunity to control the dialogue and ensure their messages are heard and that they resonate. *Jihadis* have convinced Muslims that local conflict, as well as American intervention into the Middle East, is part of a larger struggle between the West and Islam, and all Muslims are required by the *Qu'ran* to defend Islam.

f) Branding – Al-Qa'ida as an Institution. The final significant strength of Al-Qa'ida today is the *Branding* of their organization, *Al-Qa'ida*, and its rise to near institutional status worldwide. Osama Bin Laden is directly responsible for driving the organization on a successful campaign of taking what was once viewed as an allegiance-based guerilla force, into an emblem or *Brand*.[126] A *Brand* signifying an ideological banner that inspires the growth of terror cells worldwide as well as serving to influence Muslims to join the *jihad* or support the ongoing radical extremist movement. Al-Zarqawi was effective at using the brand of Al-Qa'ida in order to recruit local Iraqis to either join his organization or to provide resources and support.

The branding of Al-Qa'ida has afforded the organization the ability to inspire and influence a greater movement amongst a loose confederation of fundamentalist entities. This effort has taken precedence over internal matters such as growth, increased command and control, and resources for terror cells[127] The strategy has been successful at elevating local and regional conflicts into the greater context of Islam under siege by the West, and has catapulted Al-Qa'ida into the terror stratosphere, or the level of apocalyptic terror – willing to acquire and use weapons of mass effects-destruction.

Conversely, the *Brand* image of the United States has slowly declined over the past two decades and then plummeted as a result of the war in Iraq, as evidenced by recent survey results of the PEW Global Attitudes Project. During its most recent 2007 public opinion survey of forty-seven countries, the following was determined: 1) global support for the United States led war on terrorism continues to drop and is at its lowest since 2001, 2) the United States is the nation most often blamed for hurting the worlds environment, and 3) anti-American sentiment is continuing to rise not only in Muslim nations, but also those countries we consider our allies or friends.[128] Not only are we failing in the war of ideas in our global war on terror, but we have also lost significant ground with both the Middle East and countries and our image has suffered dramatically.

2) Al-Qa'ida Weaknesses - Vulnerabilities. Al-Qa'ida and the greater Al-Qa'ida Associated Movement (AQAM) are not without their weaknesses and like any organization or movement they have vulnerabilities that can be influenced or exploited. Critical vulnerabilities (cracks) that we must look to exploit are listed below and then

specific recommendations on how and with what means we exploit these fissures will be addressed later in this paper.

a) <u>Splintering</u>. Analysis of the Harmony documents has revealed a surprising level of infighting and conflict internal to Al-Qa'ida. Not all core members are motivated toward the same goals and predilection divergence is evident. Most notably, the influence of al-Zawahiri on bin Laden, caused the irrevocable split between bin Laden and Abdullah Azzam (cofounder of Al-Qa'ida with bin Laden), and ultimately led to the shadowy death of Azzam and his sons by unknown murderers in November 1989, one year after Al-Qa'ida had been discretely founded. Azzam and bin Laden saw two differing paths toward the creation of a greater Islamic Caliphate, and ultimately bin Laden, under significant influence by extreme Arab radical hardliners, realized that with Azzam out of the picture permanently there was no voice to counter the direction that bin Laden desired.[129]

Moreover, in Peshawar, Pakistan during the early years, friction existed in the precursor to Al-Qa'ida, the Afghan Services Bureau. The Bureau was plagued with bureaucracy problems as well as arguments over funding, resourcing, and prioritization of projects.[130] It is arguable that over time all organizations are forced to deal with friction and internal resistance. One case study of a terrorist organization may provide insight to a possible future for Al-Qa'ida. In the late 1970s in Northern Ireland, the Irish Republican Army (IRA) spawned at least six different splinter groups to include the Provisional IRA, Official IRA, Real IRA, Continuity IRA, Irish National Liberation Army (INLA), and the Catholic Reaction Force (CRF).[131] The Harmony documents have revealed significant convincing proof that significant disagreements over strategic direction and doctrine exist, and that the current loosely cohesive structure of Islamist terrorist groups is extremely tenuous.[132] Additional study and analysis of intelligence and information provided through Al-Qa'ida's media campaign and information warfare efforts, will allow us to identify further cracks and then exploit them in the future.

b) The Perpetuated Lie about Islam "In the words of a Terrorist." Islam is the worlds fastest growing religion and, since the 9/11 attacks, has come under greater scrutiny then ever before. Although there is a deliberate effort in Western culture and politics to separate terrorism from Islam, the fact that Islam is a religion of peace and tolerance, is overlooked due to the deliberate actions and messages by radical Islamist extremists, principally the *Jihadists*. Al-Qa'ida and other *Salafi-Jihadi* terrorists groups have deliberately misinterpreted and twisted the messages of the *Holy Qu'ran* and the *Sunnah* in order to rally Muslims under a banner of "Islam under Siege" and to justify their actions (violent use of terrorism and killing of innocents). Terrorism is an act against God![133] Moderate Islamic clerics and scholars state that the words of *Qu'ran* and the words of all true Muslim rulers to include the Prophet Muhammad, are that Islam forbids terrorism, and its ultimate aim is to bring peace and security to the world.[134] Unfortunately, the *Jihadis* have surreptitiously hijacked both the religion and its overt messages, by cloaking Islamic sacred cannon in a blanket of lies and hatred. *Jihadis* are currently the only voices being heard throughout the Islamic nation. A clear vulnerability for the AQAM is that Muslims condemn the actions of Islamic terror groups and their justification against the use of terror to achieve political ends is clearly against the main tenants of the religion and the teachings of the Prophet.

c) <u>The Zarqawi Effect</u>. In 1966, Abu Musab al-Zarqawi (born Ahmad Fadil Nazzal Al-Khalayleh), was born and raised in Zarqa, Jordon amidst an environment of growing Islamist activism. By the early 1990s, Jordan was overflowing with radical currents, especially those who believed in *Salafist* ideology.[135] As the country nose-dived deeper and deeper into economic and social crisis, al-Zarqawi journeyed to Afghanistan by way of Peshawar, Pakistan.[136] While in Pakistan, he was introduced to Osama bin Laden and bin Laden's mentor Abdallah Azzam. Al-Zarqawi would arrive in Afghanistan in time to see the liberation of the city of Khost and see the retreat of the defeated Soviet forces. It was also during this time he made a lasting relationship with Abu Mohammed Al-Maqdisi, who would, ultimately, assume the role of spiritual father to Zarqawi (much like Azzam was to bin Laden).[137] Upon returning to Jordon from the Soviet-Afghan War, al-Zarqawi was eventually incarcerated and his virile hatred for the "apostate" Jordanian government would grow, as would his hatred of the United States which he perceived was covertly bankrolling Jordon, thus unconditionally corrupted. The deprivation of liberty and harsh treatment in prison further convinced him of the *Salafi* path and that he was to embark on a personal journal and struggle (*Jihad*) against unbelievers, to include Christians, Jews, Shiites and Hindus.[138]

Upon returning to Afghanistan in 2000, he arrived at an Al-Qa'ida training camp in Herat along the Iranian border and far from the Taliban controlled government in Khandahar. As camp director, he surrounded himself with trusted agents and his network began to mature as did his influence over his constituents and externally. His reach went deep inside Iran, Jordan, and Iraqi Kurdistan, and he assumed the status of one of a triumvirate of leaders of Ansar al Islam, a Kurdish terrorist group based out of

Northern Iraq.[139] Following the attacks on 9/11, al-Zarqawi and Al-Qa'ida leaders met in Afghanistan one November night where he narrowly escaped death during a U.S. military missile strike. He would then proceed to flee the country with Iranian help through Iran and into Iraq.[140] It was during this time in late 2002 and early 2003, that the United States argued the case in international forums that al-Zarqawi was a legitimate link between Saddam Hussein and Al-Qa'ida, but this has never been proven and remains extremely unlikely. Ultimately, it was during late fall of 2003 and early 2004 that he emerged as the new face of terror of Al-Qa'ida in Iraq.

In October of 2004, Al-Qa'ida publicly released a letter from Zarqawi declaring *bayat*, or a pledge of loyalty to Osama bin Laden and Al-Qa'ida. He subsequently adopted the name of al-Qa'ida in Iraq (AQIZ) – *"Land of the Two Rivers."* His allegiance to bin Laden and Al-Qa'ida came about after eight months of deliberations in order to overcome serious strategic and tactical differences between bin Laden and Zarqawi. Zarqawi's personal theory was that calling for *Jihad* is not as important as actually taking action or the conduct of *Jihad* – a possible hidden subtlety and jab at scholars, especially al- Zawahiri, who were far from frontline combat and the act of engaging in *Jihad*. He also voiced that only true *mujahidin* (such as himself) took orders only from God, and not men, no matter how wise.[141] Zarqawi would quickly become the face of Al-Qa'ida as he waged a vicious terror campaign in Iraq that included beheadings, kidnappings, murder, suicide-bombings, intimidation, and eventually escalation of the conflict to incite a civil war with the *Shi'a* by overtly attacking them (civilians and militia alike). Al-Zarqawi's campaign against the *Shi'as* in Iraq was in direct contradiction of the larger Al-Qa'ida strategic theme of pragmatic alignment of all Muslims (*Sunnis and*

Shi'as), fighting together against the apostate regimes and the United States. The July 2005, highly controversial letter from al-Zawahiri to al-Zarqawi (released by the Director of National Intelligence in October 2005), rebuked the leader of AQIZ, and further exposed a fissure in the larger movement.[142] It is certain future opportunities to exploit rifts may arise as Al-Qa'ida associated groups fighting regional conflicts may have differing objectives then Al-Qa'ida strategic goals as they apply to the larger movement.

In his letter to al-Zarqawi, al-Zawahiri outlined four objectives for *Jihad* in Iraq: 1) expel the United States from Iraq (near-term), 2) establish an Islamic authority and develop it into a caliphate (short-term), exerting influence over as much of Iraq as possible, 3) extend the *Jihad* to Iraq's secular neighbors (mid-term), and 4) extend the *Jihad* to Israel (long-term).[143]

To achieve these objectives al-Zawahiri believed that the popular support of the *umma* in Iraq and neighboring countries was the most important weapon. He advised that the only way to garner popular support was to avoid acts that the *umma* does not approve of or understand (e.g., beheadings). To avoid disaffecting the *umma* he offered this counsel: 1) consult with as many factions as possible in governance and decision making, 2) minimize the excessive violence, 3) strive for unity within the *ulema* (Muslim legal scholars or those involved with Islamic studies), 4) foster unity amongst all the *mujahidin* and lastly, 5) refrain from attacking the Iraqi *Shi'as*.[144] Debatably, Al-Qai'da in Iraq has failed in all recommended objectives and has made little progress over time in advancements of al-Zawahiri's recommended strategy.

The Zarqawi - bin Laden relationship was always tenuous at best, as they each held diverging views on *Jihad*. Bin laden believed that support from the United States (far enemy) for Arab regimes in the granting of legitimacy, financing, and weapons sales were the source of these Arab governments apostate political power, therefore, he prioritized attacks against the United States. Al-Zarqawi, however, focused on the near enemy or the apostate regimes cultural and political influences within Islam, which he viewed as a clear and separate issue than support from the United States government. Eventually, both men would agree on a mutual and ultimate goal of the establishment of a true Islamic state, the caliphate, thus their relationship became one of strategic convenience where both the near and far enemy could be fought in Iraq.[145] Still, al-Zarqawi answered only to God and his ego would continue to blur his future decisions.

A prime example of al-Zarqawi's indifference to Al-Qa'ida central's guidance was the November 9, 2005, bombing attacks of three hotels in Amman, Jordan, killing 60 and wounding 115 others.[146] The attack against three American hotels, the Radisson, Grand Hyatt, and the Days Inn (all symbols of U.S. economic influence and tourism) conducted by Al-Qa'ida in Iraq *Jihadis,* was intended to inflict terror toward a larger audience, the economies, and tourism of both America and Jordon (Zarqawi's place of birth). The attack was quickly and widely condemned both in Jordan and in other Arab states, primarily because one of the bombs detonated amid a wedding party.[147] The silence that followed from Al-Qa'ida central was deafening and a clear message of tacit disapproval was apparent.

Ultimately, al-Zarqawi's days were numbered as he was unable to overcome his *takfir* and extreme *Salafi* extremist beliefs and this proved his undoing. His indiscriminate killing and use of terror tactics to coerce the *Sunnis* to align with his *Salafi-Jihadis* for fear of *Shi'a* retribution eventually backfired.

d) <u>Further Mistakes by Al-Qa'ida in Iraq</u>. On June 7, 2006, a Coalition air strike hammered its intended target and the world's most-feared terrorist, Abu Musab al-Zarqawi, lay mortally wounded. It would later come to light that his whereabouts were determined as a result of Jordanian and American intelligence collection efforts and that AQIZ had been effectively penetrated.[148] With their *emir* of Iraq killed by the hand of the infidel (American military power), AQIZ would face a dilemma in choosing their future path towards their stated goals. Should they continue their tactics of brutal attacks against the *Shi'as* and sustain martyrdom suicide operations to maintain secular conflict between *Sunnis* and *Shi'as* or should they adjust their strategy to something more in line with the approaches outlined by al-Zawahiri in his 2005 letter to Zarqawi.

Al-Qa'ida in Iraq reorganized and assumed the name of the Islamic State of Iraq (ISI) in October 2006, in an attempt to rebrand themselves and move away from the brutal tactics inspired and demanded by al-Zarqawi, and to broaden its appeal to Sunnis in Iraq as well as senior *Jihadi* scholars living outside of Iraq.[149] The paradox facing the ISI is the simple truth that they cannot control or co-opt the *Sunnis* without modifying or adapting their own ideology, and conversely, their *Jihadi* ideologues will not be satisfied unless they subject all *Sunnis* and Muslims in Iraq to Islamic law in its purist form. Abu Umar al-Baghdadi emerged as al-Zarqawi's successor and new *emir* for ISI. Claims by his followers that he was a descendant of the Prophet Muhammad were meant to further legitimize the new *emir* in the eyes of the *umma*.[150]

Nevertheless, attempts by the ISI to unite all *Sunni* insurgent factions, as well as appeal to the multiple constituencies (both inside and outside Iraq), failed miserably. On July 4, 2007, Coalition forces captured ISI's Minister of Information Khalid Umar al-

Mashadani. Consequently, he revealed that al-Baghdadi was fictitious and did not exist and that the *emir* was a fabrication to appeal to a wider Iraqi audience.[151] Not only was this a strategic blunder, it severely damaged the credibility of both ISI and Al-Qa'ida central. ISI failures have further alienated *Sunnis* and more important, have exposed vulnerabilities in the foundation of the greater Al-Qa'ida movement by the mere fact that the core Al-Qa'ida leadership can be held accountable for the actions and words of their franchises, such as ISI and other Al-Qa'ida aligned terrorist groups.

In addition to the waning appeal of ISI, the recent *Sunni Awakening* in Al Anbar Province and overt rejection of Al-Qa'ida by *Sunni* secular tribal leaders and populace is further evidence that Al-Qa'ida is far from reaching their stated objectives in Iraq.[152] Yes, Al-Qa'ida is still very active and continues to wage brutal attacks, but strategically they are losing in Iraq as the general *umma* continues to reject them and the core Al-Qa'ida leadership continues to remain aloof, almost disinterested from the ongoing *Jihad* in Iraq. What bin Laden and his *shura* council may not realize is the strategic importance of winning in Iraq. Failure by Al-Qa'ida in Iraq can be exploited not only by the West, but the entire moderate Muslim community worldwide. Through strategic communications, democratic leaders as well as Muslim leaders can articulate the failures and illegitimacy of both Al-Qa'ida and violent extremist *Salafi-Jihadism*.

e) <u>Failure in the HORN of Africa</u>. The Horn of Africa was deemed important by Al-Qaeda in the early 1990s, and combat experienced *jihadis* migrated in secrecy over several years. Al-Qa'ida fighters played a minor role in the Battle of Mogadishu in October, 1993, and saw the subsequent withdrawal of American forces. Somalia, a failed state, would appear ideal as a host for sanctuary of operatives, and would afford resources and training camps, away from Western influence and human intelligence collection. Al-Qa'ida Leadership in Afghanistan expected that Somalia would prove fertile for recruits to follow the *Salafi* ideology and wage in *Jihad* on Al-Qa'ida terms. What transpired was that many Al-Qa'ida members fell prey to extortion and betrayal. They had deep suspicions of the locals and, ultimately, found themselves caught sandwiched between immutable clan conflicts. Logistical lines of communication were hazardous and long, and the costs to run operations and training easily exceeded everyone's expectations. [153]

In the end, Al-Qa'ida failed in Somalia in the 1990s because: 1) they were mostly Arabs, and looked upon as foreigners and distrusted, 2) the African franchise failed to comprehend and work with local power structures and ignored local Islamic customs and norms, and 3) they hugely underestimated the costs of operations in a failed state with no trustworthy or supportive government. I would argue that the leadership on the ground in Somalia and also in Afghanistan failed to comprehend the nature of a tribal culture and the fact that the region was predominantly tribal and followed moderate *Sufi* Islamic teachings, and the benefits of joining a purist *Salafi* motivated *Jihad* offered nothing beneficial in return for their allegiance.

According to recent media statements by Al-Qa'ida's deputy, al-Zawahiri, Somalia is to become a new front for *Jihadis* to wage holy war against the West.[154] Knowing the past history of the region, one which is prone to terrorist attacks, as well as the past misadventures of Al-Qa'ida in Somalia, opening a new front could prove disastrous if countered by the United States and then exploited through a savvy strategic communications campaign.

f) <u>Suicide Martyrdom</u>. Addressed previously in this paper, the strategy of promoting and conducting suicide bombing against noncombatants can be argued sufficiently as un-Islamic through Islamic religious scholars and clerics. A unity of effort to include *fatwas* and edicts by clerics as well as Islamic national leaders condemning the practice, is both necessary and essential.

Current Strategic Guidance, Policies and Counterterrorism Strategies of the United States

The United States foreign policy mishaps and airline security or intelligence failures that allowed the attacks of 9/11 to occur, are beyond the scope of this project and have been well documented. In the decade that followed the collapse of the Soviet Union and defeat of communism globalization would become a major driving factor of change and the pattern became one of dynamic growth in the number of local or regional small conflicts and violent struggles. The 9/11 Commission Report correctly identified that Osama bin Laden had driven the planning and authorized the attacks, which were carried out by Islamist extremists. Khalid Sheikh Mohammed, mastermind of the original plan dubbed "the planes operation," proposed his plan to bin Laden in late 1998 or early 1999.[155] The commission also identified that the enemy is not "terrorism," but rather that it is the specific threats posed by bin Laden and others radicals who promulgate Islamist terrorism. The commission recommended that a global strategy be developed that should include the following objectives: First, attack terrorists and their organizations, second, prevent the continued growth of Islamist Terrorism and third, protect against and prepare for terrorist attacks.[156] The commission also highlighted that there must exist a unity of effort and a common set of goals across the government and thus recommended five specific areas for improvement:

1) Unify strategic intelligence and operational planning against Islamist terrorists across foreign-domestic lines with the standup of a National Counterterrorism Center.

2) Unify the strategic intelligence community with a new National Intelligence Director to oversee the national intelligence agencies and centers in order to promote unity of effort for information sharing.

3) Unify the many participants and increase information availability by implementing a network-based information system that overcomes traditional stovepipe systems.

4) Unify congressional oversight to improve accountability and quality of work.

5) Strengthen the FBI and homeland defenders.[157]

These recommendations became invaluable as the Bush administration worked quickly to implement as well as make visible changes in the Homeland Security – Homeland Defense, Intelligence, and counterterrorism areas. Militarily, the United States responded quickly, and deployed special operations forces, air power, as well as limited conventional forces. Partnered with Northern Alliance Afghanis, the Taliban was swiftly defeated and Al-Qa'ida *Jihadis* were forced to either die while fighting or exfiltrate and fight another day. Al-Qa'ida central, after a brief time in the Tora Bora region of Southeast Afghanistan, quietly slipped away across the border and into Pakistan, where they are believed to be today operating out of the federally administered tribal areas (FATA), well protected amongst friendly tribes. But not resting on success in Afghanistan, the administration rode this wave and quickly oriented on Iraq, deploying forces that attacked in March 2003, to topple Saddam Hussein and the *Sunni Baathist* Regime.

Now going on five years of fighting in Iraq and also a heavy commitment to counterinsurgency and nation-building in Afghanistan, the United States is still a very long-way from achieving the recommended goal by the 9/11 commission of preventing the growth of Islamist terrorism. Conversely, direct intervention into the Muslim world (OPERATION IRAQI FREEDOM) has exponentially elevated both the stature and support for radical Islamists. Additionally, blunders with significant strategic impact and blowback (Abu Ghraib scandal and Guantanomo Bay detainments debates), has inadvertently furthered the Al-Qa'ida agenda and inspired a new generation of *Jihadis*. Equally important is the slow realization that although we have recently published a National Security Strategy (2006), National Strategy for Combating Terrorism (2006), and National Military Strategy for the War on Terrorism (2006), all are lacking in detail and direction with regards to the formulation of a Grand National Strategy to defeat Al-Qa'ida and the Islamist terrorist movement it has inspired.

The major criticisms of our current national strategy on combating terrorism are threefold. First, the term Global War on Terror (GWOT) is extremely inadequate in articulating the war we need to fight, which is a combined effort to defeat Al-Qa'ida and its movement. We are certainly not fighting every possible terrorist group worldwide (such as the Basque nationalists) but rather, the groups we have to prioritize our resources and strategic thinking against are the radical Islamist Terrorists, of which Al-Qa'ida reign supreme. Moreover, the masterful strategic communications campaign of our true enemy, Al Qa'ida, has manipulated our GWOT diatribe into a global war against Islam, which has done more damage then we could have predicted.

The second major criticism of our National Strategy for Combating Terrorism is that we have grossly erred in assuming that the advancement of effective democracies in the Middle East is the long term antidote to the ideology of terrorism.[158] Terrorism is a tactic. *Salafism, Qutbism,* and *Wahhabism* are ideologies that inspire radical Islamist groups to use terror as a means to advance their political agendas in order to achieve their stated ends. Our public diplomacy and national strategies emphasizing *"bringing democracy"* to Islamic societies is seen as self-serving duplicity by Muslims of the Middle East. American messages of "Promote Freedom" are considered patronizing and suggest that Arabs are enslaved and without sufficient human rights. Furthermore, in the minds of Muslims the "occupations" of Afghanistan and Iraq have not led to democracy, but have led to chaos, suffering, and greater instability.[159]

The final criticism of our strategy to combat terror is that we have identified national objectives, but have failed to develop a comprehensive supporting and enduring strategy to achieve them. Efforts are not fully synchronized and, although we have made significant changes in our bureaucracy since the 9/11 attacks, more are needed. What we lack is a Grand National Strategy against Al-Qa'ida and Islamist Extremists. A Grand Strategy that would provide not only purpose but, more importantly ends, ways, means as well as direction, lines of operation, outline prioritization of resources, and establish a unity of effort amongst all branches of government to include cabinets, agencies, departments, and Congress. The remainder of this paper will present several initiatives for consideration to be implemented in the development of a Grand National Strategy and Integrated Long War Campaign Plan with the goal of defeating Al-Qa'ida, The Al-Qa'ida Associated Movement and *Salafi-Jihadi* Terrorist Organizations, and containing Islamist extremism.

<u>Initiatives for Grand National Strategy and Campaign Planning in the War against Al-Qa'ida, the Al-Qa'ida Associated Movement and Islamist Terrorism.</u>

Grand National Strategy and Campaign Design-Planning.

From the start, we must clearly understand that a war on terror will have no end date in the future – terror is a tactic and not an entity unto itself. We are better served by identifying the right enemy or threat, and design a strategy and campaign to destroy, defeat, or contain that threat. Deterrence strategies may work against supporters of terror cells, but have proven ineffective against hard-line radical extremists. The primary terrorist threats the United States must focus on and direct our resources against are Al-Qa'ida, the larger Al'-Qa'ida Associated Movement (AQAM) of *Salafi-Jihadi* Terrorist Organizations, and Islamist terrorists. Three critical assumptions are needed with respect to the threats:

- Al-Qa'ida will not quietly abandon the *jihad* nor will they negotiate for peace.

- Al-Qa'ida will continue to approve or conduct terror attacks and 4th generation warfare methods, as opposed to man, train, and equip a conventional force.

- Al-Qa'ida will continue to adapt and evolve. They will exploit all of their capability to conduct destruction and they will not self-impose limits (they have openly and covertly stated they intend to acquire WMD-WME).[160]

Our best approach, as far as entering into a long-war mindset against the threat, is to look at this from the same perspective as we did for five decades over the span of the Cold War. The Soviet Union and our individual fear over the unchecked spread of communism galvanized our country and our government. In short, the Cold War was a fifty year long-term multidimensional struggle against an insidious and violent ideology (Communism).[161] We absolutely must leverage the near, mid and long terms threats that Al-Qa'ida, Islamist terrorists and Islamist extremist ideologies pose to our vital national interests and way of life. We must stand firmly and galvanize ourselves and emulate our forefathers with the same resolve as previous generations. The attacks of 9/11 shattered our illusion of a post Cold War indolent tranquility. The stakes today could not be higher as Al-Qa'ida will not stop unless they are stopped. They are fighting a war of exhaustion and attrition of our willpower. A long-war mindset must permeate everyone involved with strategy development and campaign design if we have any chance of success.

Grand National Strategy development must start with the digestion of the current national strategies for National Security, Homeland Security, and Combating Terror, then the integration of an updated National Defense Strategy, National Military Strategy, and Military Strategic Plan for the War on Terrorism, and then assessed against a comprehensive in-depth top to bottom study of the Islamist terrorism threats, ideology, capability, and their strategic objectives. Only after this comprehensive and detailed analysis is done, can we begin to identify and build our Grand National Strategy. A synergistic and holistic strategy that provides direction, and ensures symmetry between achievable and compatible ends, concepts, means, resources, and the policies required to achieve those ends. The team charged with developing the strategy must be comprehensive and include military planners, experts from all parts of the government, academicians and scholars, social movement theory experts, think tank – regional -

cultural experts, as well as senior leadership throughout the process since this will need to be an iterative process of development with refinements.

Can we win or achieve victory once we develop a Grand Strategy? We must first define what victory should look and on what conditions. Ultimate victory in a war against Islamist terrorism will come only when the violent extremist ideology has been countered and undermined, when those who have pledged fealty to Al-Qa'ida to destroy the United States and our way of life have been killed, captured, or coerced to abandon their cause. Victory will not mean the end of terrorism or acts of terror. Osama bin Laden must know he will never achieve his vision of a greater Islamic caliphate from Morocco to Central Asia. That he will not live to see the United States abandon the Middle East, or see Israel destroyed in his lifetime. That evil will not triumph over good.

Campaign design at the national level while currently fighting on two major fronts can be achieved. We have the benefit of knowing our adversary first hand, as well as seven years of experience with both operational and tactical lessons learned. One bureaucratic change that is needed immediately is the creation of a position within our government that can oversee the development, implementation, and execution of the Grand Strategy. A position empowered to cross all branches of government and provide purpose, assign tasks, and give direction, and yet be accountable to both the executive and legislative branches. A Vice President of War might fulfill the requirement. One, who answers to the President and Congress, has regulatory authority written in law, whose overarching responsibility is to oversee the long war against Islamist terrorism and that all aspects of government are executing their requirements and their efforts are synchronized.

1) <u>Strategic Objectives</u>. Strategic objectives must be identified early in the process and throughout the duration of war, and reassessed and adjusted over time as new enemies and threats emerge. We must also plan far enough out through a lens that identifies objectives in the Immediate, Near-Term, Mid-Term, and Far-Term horizons. A simple example of objectives nested over time follows:

Strategic Objectives

    Line of Operation (Enemy Leadership and Forces)

    - Immediate (1-2 Years)

        - Disrupt Al-Qa'ida (Core) Command, Control and Communications

        - Destroy ISI (Al-Qa'ida in Iraq)

        - Destroy any Islamist Terror Cell who acquires/uses WMD

        - Disrupt any AQAM attacks in the Homeland

        - Contain *Sunni* Islamist Terrorist groups

        - Discredit AQAM ideologies

    - Near-Term (2-7 Years)

        - Destroy Al-Qa'ida Core Command and Control (and leaders)

        - Destroy *Sunni Salafi-Jihadi* Terror Group C2-leaders

        - Attrit AQAM leadership/C2

        - Disrupt AQAM network linkages

        - Destroy Al-Qa'ida Brand – Improve Brand America

    - Mid-Term (7-15 Years)

        - Destroy AQAM leadership/C2

        - Defeat Islamist Terror Cells

- Far-Term (15-40 Years)

- Destroy – Neutralize Islamist Terror Cells

2) <u>Where to fight</u>. The Grand National Strategy and supporting campaign plan will identify several operational fronts on which to focus and where to apply resources. Each front will fall under a geographical combatant commands' responsibility to enhance unity of command. To maximize the full interagency approach to war against terrorist groups, senior interagency positions within the COCOMs will be manned with quality and experienced personnel. An ambassador-at-large or Senior State Department service member position under the COCOM Commander should also be considered, as the war will be fought using the full complement of national power to include soft and hard power. The immediate priority operational fronts to conduct counterterror operations against Islamist terrorists should orient on where our intelligence indicates there are existing terror cells or where areas are that could emerge as hosts or recruiting grounds of Islamist terrorist organizations, specifically the AQAM. The following should be considered:

a) <u>Iraq</u>. A new and updated strategy for Iraq is required. One that reduces the forces on the ground, yet does not undercut the growth and improvements of the Iraqi security forces. A strategy that integrates other Muslim and Arabic countries security forces with a smaller U.S. military force footprint. The targeting and eventual destruction of the Islamic State of Iraq and any or all *Sunni* Islamist terrorist organizations is of the utmost priority. COIN and nation-building are imperative for long-term stability and the United States along with other UN partners to include the Republic of China and Russia, must ante up and help. Current Coalition COIN efforts are being undermined because of the limited availability of civil reconstruction and governance expertise. Collapse in Iraq would be a monumental setback to United States foreign policy as well as have a serious impact on the price of oil, therefore, negatively affecting world economies. This mutual interest must be leveraged for commitments by other nations to see through the stability of Iraq until the country can secure and govern itself without external or internal threat to its survival.

b) Afghanistan – Pakistan. A significant strategy revision is required. One that addresses Pakistan and Afghanistan as interconnected and part of a larger problem set. When developing objectives and approaches it is crucial to look at nation-building, economic prosperity, and feasible options to reduce the reliance on drug trade profits, thereby undercutting the funding of the current Taliban insurgency. Our revised strategy will combine both soft and hard power along nation-state lines, as well as historical tribal lines when appropriate.

c) HORN of Africa. Currently a supporting effort and as mentioned earlier, attempts by Al-Qa'ida to grow franchises in the HORN in the 1990s, as well as setup training camps, proved to be extremely difficult. Still, the HORN of Africa remains an extremely unstable area and the Muslim population continues to escalate through conversions and increased birth-rates. A strategy for the HORN would likely rely on resources committed through a theater security cooperation plan under a COCOM control, as well as multinational IGO, NGO humanitarian efforts, and through regional security organizations. If actionable intelligence is available on existing terror cells, then discrete operations or low visibility strikes by either special operations forces or unmanned aircraft should be used to defeat those elements. Somalia and Kenya must be closely monitored for both are fertile and chaos exists in both countries. Significant

resources towards growth of human intelligence capabilities in the HORN are required

as well as the time necessary to slowly and safely build, and then safeguard, and exploit

reliable HUMINT networks.

d) Europe. Current projections are that by the year 2010, twenty to twenty-

five percent of all workers in Europe will be Muslims. By 2050, the current Muslim

population (estimated 16-30 million) will double in size.[162] European birth rates have

reached all-time lows as countries find they are at a critical turning point, and could see

their indigenous populations drop by as much as half by the end of the twenty-first

century.[163] Eastern Europeans are migrating to Western Europe while Muslims are both

immigrating and reproducing second and third generations thereby, altering the religious

makeup in the West. Britain, which has an estimated 1.6 million Muslims, is

approaching a crossroads with respect to its foreign and domestic policies. The 7/7

Bombings, London public transport suicide bombings on July 7, 2005, which killed 52

civilians and wounded another 700, was archetypal of an Al-Qa'ida planned

simultaneous attack. A simultaneous attack intended to terrorize a larger audience and

achieve a mass psychological effect on Londonites and Britons.[164] Al-Qa'ida would

ultimately claim responsibility for the attack and the revelation that the suicide bombers

were all British citizens clearly indicated the gravity of the situation with regards to terror

cells growing from within. London was eerily similar to the 2004 suicide bombings in

Madrid, Spain which killed 191, and injured over 1700 civilians.[165] The salient point

being that the number of terror attacks by Islamist-motivated groups is rising in Europe.

That fact combined with a significant growth of Muslims who are not truly integrated into

European societies, is a recipe for disaster. Undoubtedly, there still remains holdover *Jihadis* from the Bosnian War which could serve as catalysts to increasing the intensity of Al-Qa'ida or Islamist terrorist attacks. Europe is a vital front where the United States must work closely with our European friends, and utilize our soft power resources to maximum advantage and mutual benefit.

e) <u>Middle East</u>. A broad front that would require an even broader strategy, heavily reliant on soft vice hard power. The United States must look to reduce our overt military presence in the region, yet stay very connected to remain in a position to influence. Working to renew the *"Brand American"* by not only our words but our deeds. We must drop the democracy dialogue and then embark to gain better footing to communicate strategically with multiple target audiences. It is within the Middle Eastern countries that the Islamist scholars live, from which the *Salafists* and *Jihadis* draw their ideology. The Middle East holds the heart of Islam, therefore, we must target this region methodically and in such a manner so as not to inadvertently rejuvenate the *Jihadis* or give them more reason to inspire recruits and resources. Moderates do exist, and we must seek them out and allow their voice to resonate in order to counter the messages of extremism and hate.

f) <u>Southeast Asia</u>. Another complex front consisting of two separate and distinct geographic regions. On the mainland, consisting of Cambodia, Laos, Myanmar, Thailand, and Vietnam where Buddhism is the primary religion, a strategy of building relationships and long term partnerships to prevent future Islamist terrorist intervention, is necessary. While in the maritime countries of Brunei, East Timor, Malaysia, the Philippines, Singapore, and Indonesia, Islam is the dominate religion. The seeds of Al-

Qa'ida are already growing in Indonesia, one of the largest areas of concentrated Muslims, as the Bali bombings would indicate. To date, this front has been an economy of effort and must be prioritized higher and resourced, before Al-Qa'ida establishes strong roots and grows franchises that have global reach capabilities. Expanded HUMINT capabilities will have to grow over time and be safeguarded.

g) <u>The Homeland and North America</u>. The security of our homeland and of our people will always be a vital national interest of our government. Significant improvements within the establishment, organizations and the standup of the Homeland Security Department have occurred since 9/11. Yet, we cannot protect and defend everything and not everything is a legitimate target of strategic value to our enemy. Our financial and transportation sectors are most vulnerable and would have the greatest economic impact on both the United States economy but also the world. A detailed review of our policies and objectives for homeland security must be undertaken, and then over the duration of the long war campaign, we can adjust the proper amount of resources in the actual defense of the homeland. We can create certain efficiencies by eliminating some of the multiple bureaucracies that currently exist, once decisions are made after the Grand National Strategy and supporting campaign plan are developed, approved and then implemented.

Reorganizing to Fight a Campaign Against Al-Qa'ida, the Al-Qa'ida Associated Movement and Islamist Terrorism.

Although we have counterterrorism experts in several departments of government as well on the National Security Council team, we still lack and need a single individual and organization to both orchestrate and oversee our Counterterrorism

Grand National Strategy and Integrated Long War Campaign Plan. As previously

mentioned, a Vice President of War is offered for consideration.

Equally important, we need to enter into the discourse on how to study and

research terrorism, or more specifically Islamist terrorism. At a minimum, a more holistic

approach that incorporates systems thinking to include epistemological, politics, social

movement theory, and theology is required. Terrorism researchers and analysts are

often handicapped by methodical or problem-solving approaches; much like the

American military's dogmatic approach to centers of gravity and critical thinking. It is

nearly impossible to predict Al-Qa'ida's next strategic moves, but it is still important to

try. One rule that is helpful to understand when conducting strategic and operational

analysis with respect to Al-Qa'ida is this: In *Al-Qa'ida Math* it is not important that two

plus two will always equal four, (it does not). What is important is that two plus two in *Al

Qa'ida Math* equates to something between three and five. We require strategies that

reflect both strategic and operational art, as opposed to purely scientific and methodical

approaches. As we move forward in this century, the United States will require a

coherent, resourced and synchronized Terrorism Grand National Strategy that is

focused on the correct adversaries and against all possible outcomes in order to

counter-their strategies and defeat them.

1) Mobilize the Government. The United States Special Operations Command

(USSOCOM) is currently the lead for the Department of Defense in the war on

terrorism. Although a significant positive step forward in the aftermath of 9/11,

USSOCOM has no written or legal authority to direct other components of the

interagency to take action or conduct SOCOM directed tasks. Instead, they rely on efforts to compel, co-opt, or convince other elements of the interagency through fostering a sense of unity of effort. Arguably the CIA, Department of Defense, Department of State, and Department of Homeland Security organizations and personnel have carried the heaviest loads since the attacks of 9/11. A common condemnation from both the Iraq and Afghanistan frontlines is that unit commanders desperately needed financial, agricultural, electrical – energy, Justice and State Department subject matter experts to provide them the much needed know-how in stabilization and reconstruction operations. A generally acknowledged maxim from the British classical counterinsurgency experience is that to defeat an insurgency, it is about one quarter military and three quarters something else (implying soft power, money, nation building, and reconstruction). Mobilization of all facets of our government is long overdue and funding and resources are needed to grow and build capacity where it is urgently needed and where it is currently under-resourced.

Al-Qa'ida presents a very real omnipotent and present danger, yet curiously enough, our federal government has enacted only minor changes and improvements to overcome its own inherent bureaucracy (a weakness noted in the 9/11 Commission report). The underlying principle problem is we have yet fully realized that military force alone, is insufficient at destroying Al-Qa'ida nor is it sufficient to defeat the associated movement of terror and impending global insurgency. USSOCOM is a vital component to the effort, but a higher authority is needed to ensure synchronization and prioritization across the interagency is achieved. The traditionally domestically focused federal agencies must be transformed and integrated into the larger effort to include policy development that is directly related to counterterrorism efforts. To wage war now and in the future against Al-Qa'ida and other Islamist terrorist organizations, we must develop a balanced and integrated approach that uses both soft and hard power methods to achieve results through a campaign plan approach.

Here are but two examples of untapped capabilities that could be beneficial in the fight against terror. The United States Customs and Border Protection (CBP) now falls under the Department of Homeland Security. Recognized as experts in border management, fraudulent document detection, and maritime security, CBP could provide much-needed training for our multinational partners to assist in border security, and make significant improvements in recognition and detainment of *Jihadis* attempting to infiltrate certain countries. Numerous captured *Jihadis* under interrogation have provided detailed accounts of their movement to hotspots, and once these trends and patterns are identified, we should leverage the CBPs expertise and work with those countries most needing the help. Another example, the Department of Energy (DOE) is being overlooked with the ongoing counterinsurgency in Iraq. DOE maintains numerous partner and capability building capacities, as well as expertise in areas such as energy efficiency, refinery planning and repair, and electrical planning expertise.[166] My experiences in both al-Fallujah in 2003-2004 and Baghdad in 2005-2006, clearly highly for me and my unit the importance of much needed expertise in this sector for both the National, Provincial and local levels of Iraqi ministry essential services. Al-Qa'ida appeals to those *Sunnis* who are disenfranchised and lack of power, pay high black market gas prices and have experienced rising costs of food, is a direct result of the inability of the Iraqi government to manage essential services, and our inadequate resourcing of experts and expertise to help Iraqis solve their problems.

2) <u>Long-War Mindset</u>. A long war campaign against Islamist terrorism is not a sprint, nor is it a marathon, but is quite possibly several back to back and overlapping marathons with short sprints interwoven. We cannot overextend ourselves too early for fear of real fatigue. Our ground forces are closest to breaking right now as they continue to conduct back to back deployments, with minimum dwell times at home. Our brigade combat teams in many cases will return for a third or possibly a fourth deployment in the 2008 through 2010 time frame. Maintaining our current pace with our current force strength authorizations will border dangerously on the cusp of a potential collapse of the all-volunteer Army. There exists no better time than now to expand our military landpower end-strength and to transform select formations to focus on the irregular and long war ahead that faces us, and accept risk in other areas such as the procurement of extremely expensive equipment, like the future combat system. We will always need to maintain a highly trained deployable finishing force as was the case in OPERATIONs DESERT STORM and IRAQI FREEDOM I, but we can move to a more balanced force and fight the war that needs fighting and the type of war the enemy will fight against us, while simultaneously maintaining a smaller, highly lethal capability in the event a true peer competitor comes along with the motivation to directly fight the United States in a high intensity conflict. It is much more likely we will fight a 5th-generational warfare force in a form of hybrid warfare, where our enemy will utilize a mix of conventional and irregular methods to achieve his desired effects.

3) <u>United States Special Operations Command (USSOCOM)</u>. The USSOCOM has developed a classified version of a long war campaign plan in support of the global war on terror. However, as addressed earlier, USSOCOM is not in a position to direct

other elements of the interagency as well as task government agencies outside the span of control of the Department of Defenses to execute certain functions with respect to implementing all elements of national power. I propose that the USSOCOM campaign plan be the groundwork for a much needed interagency effort (Integrated Long War Campaign Plan – ILWCP) that supports a well-developed and applicable Grand National Strategy. The result would be a wide-ranging comprehensive ILWCP aimed directly at Al-Qa'ida, the Al-Qa'ida Associated Movement, and Islamist terrorists (*Jihadis*) and executed through the combined and coordinated application of diplomatic, informational, military instruments of national power supported through a unified interagency effort in partnership with multinational friends and allies, a variety of international governmental organizations, non-governmental organizations, and regional security organizations.

4) <u>Bipartisan Support for the ILWCP and Enduring Foreign Policy</u>. Bipartisan commitment and support is essential and should be demanded with respect to developing a cohesive strategy and multi-dimensional campaign. The nature of a comprehensive and integrated campaign plan is that it endures over time, with minor adjustments or mid-course corrections and, as events occur, the objectives and end state remain relatively unchanged. Future administrations must accept the process and product since consistency is an underlying theme we need to drive both within the United States and across the world. A common criticism of the United States today is the perception by non-Americans that our political parties and their diverging agendas tend to drive the national agenda. That, in addition to the fact that historically when every new administration arrives to the White House, the first real crisis that occurs

causes major changes to a previously recognized foreign policy. The execution of the ILWCP against Al-Qa'ida, AQAM and Islamist terrorist organizations will undoubtedly be long, have dark moments as well as breakthroughs, and require immense willpower and resources throughout as we endeavor to exhaust our enemy, and counter his efforts to exhaust us.

American military forces and the Department of Defense will continue to play a dominant role and remain a significant partner in the greater interagency effort to prosecute the ILWCP. Nevertheless, we must also be cognizant of the fact that overuse of military force and/or presence in the Middle East can run the risk of further stirring anti-American sentiments and worsening our *Brand* appeal, as well as be strategically used against us through Al-Qa'ida's strategic communications expertise.

Join in and Fight in "The War of Ideas"

If we were to conduct an opinion poll worldwide about the war of ideologies (Democracy versus Islamist Terrorism), we would find our efforts have fallen far short of our desired results and, more important we are losing while simultaneously falling back and giving up ground. The Internet has largely served its part as multiplier of radical ideologies, and has changed the nature of Islamist movement participation, since one no longer needs to physically relocate to support a specific activist cause, but can do so from anywhere at anytime through a computer.[167] More resources and thought must be put toward better understanding the ideologies that Islamist terrorists espouse and the vulnerabilities of the Al-Qa'ida ideology.

One ingredient that holds the greater Al-Qa'ida system together is the shared hatred of apostasy. This hatred metastasizes into unrefined power, new recruits, funding, and the overt and covert support of other states, while serving to motivate *Jihadists* to wage their brand of asymmetric warfare. Apostate regimes (Jordan, Egypt, Saudi Arabia, et cetera) are openly blamed for causing poverty, corruption, allowing the spread of Western influences at the expense of Islam, and social and political repression.

1) <u>American Interests, Values and the Democracy Agenda</u>. American foreign policy is driven by a combination of national interests and our deeply rooted values. Although our interests have changed over time since our Founding Fathers authored the Constitution, our values have remained relatively constant. Great nations arrive and survive over time not solely on military strength or economic prosperity, but because of their ideals and values and their commitment to them. Freedom is the overriding value that defines America and Americans. Our National Security Strategy outlines that in order to lay the foundations of future peace we must promote freedom and democracy as an alternative to tyranny and despair.[168] Our current strategy is founded on two pillars:

- Promote freedom, justice, and human dignity – working to end tyranny, to promote effective democracies, and to extend prosperity through free and fair trade and wise development policies.

- Confront the challenges of our time by leading a growing community of democracies.[169]

The ideological gaffe we continue to make is that our strategic leadership is developing strategy in the same mindset that we used when confronted with Communism, our greatest threat to our way of life in the past half-century. We fail to understand that democracy is no longer an effective deterrent or inspirational motivator for states and non-state actors in the post Cold-War world, especially in the Middle East. Islamic activists believe democracy threatens Islam while Islamic extremists emphasize that perception in order to galvanize support throughout the greater Islamic nation. Moreover, the track record of democratic growth during the Bush administrations tenure is abysmal when seen through the eyes of Muslims, especially those in the Middle East and the heart of the Islam. American interventions into Somalia, Afghanistan and now Iraq have resulted only in chaos, anarchy, further enforcing the belief that those who push democracy are in competition with deeply rooted Muslim historical traditions. To overcome this perception and regain credibility amongst Muslims everywhere, I argue that we should omit "Democratization" and "Freedom Agenda" from our strategic communications and public diplomacy lexicon when orienting on Islamism and Islamist terrorist groups.

2) ReBranding America. Our *ReBranding* of America strategy must focus on our values (human dignity, justice, freedom of choices) should be central to our strategic messages. We can continue to promote that we favor representative governments that exist for their peoples, but accept the fact that governments do not have to be democratic to be good and protective of their constituents. Countering Al-Qa'ida's fundamental argument that democracy is a threat to Islam off the table, would afford us greater advantage when working to counter their ideals of a utopian society shrouded under the cloak of Islam.

The United States was once heralded and known worldwide as a beacon of freedom; a country that epitomized freedom, hope, and dignity. Our leaders urged all nations to comply with international treaties and work hard to initiate social reforms in order to protect human rights and civil liberties. But, as of late, we have oft abandoned our own message, and have failed to sign treaties, or in some cases, follow international laws. In addition, the international repercussions from the scandals of Abu Ghraib and Guantanamo Bay have further damaged our credibility worldwide, leaving us much more work to do to in order to regain legitimacy in the eyes of others. We must reorient ourselves and our messages, in order to truly engage in a war of ideals and competing ideologies. I am not a proponent of throwing out democracy, just the opposite. However, I believe we are better served by not overtly pushing democratization, but to promote our long standing values, work with governments of all types to improve civil liberties and who embrace the same values as ours in order to create the environment where others once again aspire to be like America, or to come to this great nation. Good triumphs over evil. Developing United States foreign policy will continue to be a delicate balance of idealism and realism but, framing a long war approach against Islamist terrorism that is built upon our American values and embraces the peaceful messages of Islam, will become essential.

     3) <u>Defeat the Al-Qa'ida Ideology (Core Strength of AQAM)</u>. Ideologies can be discredited by failure. The war against Al-Qa'ida will continue to be fought on the physical battlefield, but we must take the offensive in the psychological battlefield as well. Central to this is attacking and discrediting the logic and ideology of Al-Qa'ida first, and then influencing the ideologies of other Islamist terror groups and exploiting their vulnerabilities in order to separate them from the greater populace that they must have

in order to survive and win. Five principal objectives are necessary to defeat the logic of Islamist terrorism:

a) Expose Al-Qa'ida's ideological inconsistencies with the *Qu'ran* and the *Sunnah*. Discredit their extremist ideology and dissuade its appeal to mainstream Muslims. *Salafism*, *Qutbism*, *Wahhabism* are all different interpretations of *Qu'ran* and the Sunnah, and no one single ideology is infallible. Many of these extremists' interpretations of Islam can be directly attacked and countered by *Qu'ranic* verse. *Salafi Jihadists* and their extremist views are often averse to traditional Muslim practices and have openly declared other sects within Islam to be heretics, most prominently the *Sufis*.[170] This is one of many themes or acts that can be discredited. Governments in Saudi Arabia, Jordan, and Algeria have conducted successful domestic information programs to attack and discredit *Salafi* themes, but this effort must be expanded to beyond the domestic audiences in order to attack a transnational foe. No one body is empowered to speak for Islam, therefore, a strong body of voices must surface amongst the more moderate Islamic clerics and scholars with the religious credentials or "Street Cred" who could then collectively discredit the violent ideologies, while America lends support quietly, and far from sight.

b) Discredit the living guiding thinkers of the *Salafi-Jihadi* movement. Abu Muhammad al-Maqdisi (Jordan), 'Abd al-Qadir b. 'Abd al'Aziz) (Egypt), Abu Basir al-Tartusi and Abu Qatada (England), and the most extremist of Saudi clerics.[171] The best way to discredit these men is by clerics and by credible scholars with experience and the intellectual foundations within the study of Islam, the *Qu'ran* and the *Sunnah*. Exploit any Al-Qa'ida or *Salafi-Jihadist* exiles, who now oppose the path of violent extremism.

Denouncements of prominent *Jihadis* by other prominent *Jihadis* is extremely damaging as well as demoralizing to the entire group and movement.[172]

By labeling the entire Al-Qa'ida *Jihadi* movement ideology as *Qutbism* (Qutb is most often cited amongst Al-Qa'ida writings), we can better orient on that ideology's vulnerable points that can be attacked and then exploited. Muslims must understand that *Jihadis* seek to implement a totalitarian system in which no individual is allowed to think for themselves.[173] Reminding Muslims what happens when *Jihadis* come to power is paramount. The previous conditions during the Taliban led Afghanistan, with all of its problems and repression and loss of individual freedoms, is intractable truth of what lies ahead for supporters of *Salafi*-inspired *Jihad*.

c) A convincing alternative to Al-Qa'ida and *Salafi-Jihadi* ideologies must be available for Islamic activists and mainstream Muslims. Moderate Muslim dialogue and religious interpretation must become louder and more widespread then the current rhetoric filled with hatred and violence. The United States could assume a supporting effort as opposed to a leading role in partnership with Muslim scholars, ideologues, academics, clerics, and Arab – Islamic regime leaders to set conditions for more moderate views of reform to be heard. By isolating, discrediting, attacking, and countering Al-Qa'ida's ideological appeal while providing other non-violent alternatives, is one primary method to achieve this objective.

d) Discredit the Al-Qa'ida inspired *Jihad* as a *Holy War* in the name of Islam. According to the classical interpretation of the *Qu'ran*, the notion of *Jihad* refers to a noble human struggle to realize God's will for a just and merciful society on earth and for the individual to uphold what is good and resist what is evil. *Jihad* comes from the root word *jahada* (to strive for self-betterment from a moral-ethical perspective).[174] A

thousand years of Islamic jurisprudence has provided us a better word, to counter or un-

jihad. As Layla Seain of the Association of Muslim Scientists explains:

"*Hirabah* comes from the root word *hariba* (to fight, to go to war or become

enraged or angry), an etymological and theological examination of these words provide

a valid framework through which the religious legitimacy of suicide bombings in today's

global community can be examined. To delve into comparative study of these Islamic

contexts, is to expose how *hirabah* is being paraded by terror groups as *jihad*. By

defining *hirabah* as *jihad*, Al-Qa'ida and other terrorist groups promote their agendas by

misleading young, religiously motivated and impressionable Muslims that killing

unarmed and non-combatant civilians are activities of *Jihad*, hence a ticket to

paradise."[175]

Emphasizing that Al-Qa'ida is conducting *Hirabah* instead *Jihad* would discredit

them amongst the Islamic people they are working to influence. Islamic religious

authorities must be the body of individuals that collectively discredit Al-Qa'ida's war for

any chance of success of Muslims accepting that Al-Qa'ida is not fighting a just and holy

war, but is waging a campaign of murder against mankind and that their fighters are not

mujahidin, but are murderers. Muslims believe that if fighters are not *mujahidin* they will

not die as martyrs (*shahiddin*) and they will only bring their family disgrace and not

glory. They will bring hardship to Muslims everywhere. Any act to support Al-Qa'ida's

Jihad, would not glorify Allah, but subsequently defile him.

e) Study the *Qu'ran* to counter the Al-Qa'ida False Messages. Islamic

sacred canon was never intended to be an accurate account of world history, but was meant to deliver the compelling message of God's revelation to man.[176] Stories were written not to establish what actually happened, but to serve over time as lessons of meaning, identity, and a greater sense of belonging, therefore – sacred meanings.[177] Clerics must lead in this effort as opposed to government leaders, in order to maintain legitimacy in the minds of Muslims. The simple truth, that Al-Qa'ida is responsible for more Muslim deaths by supporting sectarian violence in Iraq then all of the Western countries combined, must be forefront on the agenda in order to further discredit the organization. The West cannot challenge *Salafism* intellectually as we lack the cultural background, experience, and credibility amongst the audience we are targeting to influence, the greater Muslim people. We will need the help of other influential Muslims.

f) <u>Positive Themes to Enforce</u>. While simultaneously discrediting Al-Qa'ida and their ideology, we must also increase our efforts along the lines of promoting positive themes. Globalization has provided the conditions for a revival in Islam. The primary issue that *Salafi-Jihadis* have used to mobilize support is that modernity is a threat to Islam, therefore, we (Muslims) return to a more puritanical and repressive society, where *shari'a* is the only law. We must engender an approach that deflects the *Salafi* argument, and that builds upon a premise that modernity and Islam can coexist and benefit from one another. With modernity comes information and technological advances that provide information to greater audiences. Improvements in water purification, energy distribution, or agriculture, which result in better food and more reliable basic services, come as the result of advances in technology and modernity and subsequently benefit all Muslims. Al-Qa'ida offers only what the Taliban offered, fiefdom, strict autocratic rule, repression, poverty, and a significant loss of civil liberties and freedom of choice. Muslims have choices and a moderate voice and interpretation to embrace modernity will have to evolve from the Middle East. Our role is to help influence and stimulate these voices. Muslims should be empowered with the knowledge to reject the radical interpretation that Islamic canon is closed to interpretation. Credible and respected mainstream clerics who issue *fatwas* are essential to counter Al-Qa'ida's radical Islamist interpretations and themes.

g) <u>Sustain the Offensive in the Ideological Fight with Al-Qa'ida and *Salafi Jihadis*</u>. To achieve the five objectives highlighted previously to counter the logic of Islamist terrorism, we must maintain an offensive mindset that endures over time. However, we must comprehend that we are better served to wage the war of ideas by selective direct confrontation and indirectly through other parties. American Muslims are our greatest ally, and that can be leveraged to overcome a perception that America is against Islam. At times, we may need to be ruthless by co-opting or coercing individuals to denounce Al-Qa'ida and the *Salafi-Jihadi* ideology. Our Grand National Strategy must identify both overt and covert components, ways and means, in order to achieve our immediate, near, mid and long-term objectives. If left unchecked, or if we assume only a defensive posture against terror organizations, Islamic fundamentalism will continue to spread and terror groups will spread their ideologies and further embed themselves into Muslim societies and quite possibly lead us towards an apocalyptic global clash between civilizations.

Identify and Exploit Strategic Opportunities

Undoubtedly, opportunities of strategic significance will emerge and then disappear throughout the waging of the Integrated Long War Campaign (ILWCP) against Al-Qa'ida. Unfortunately, we have missed several that have been available to exploit, while Islamist terrorists have proven worthy adversaries at their ability to exploit our mishaps, such as Abu Ghraib. The following are examples of opportunities that either have been overlooked by the West, or that we must endeavor to exploit in the future.

　　　1) <u>Fadl and the Recantation of Violence in the name of Islam</u>. In November 2007, leading Egyptian *Jihadist* Sayyid Imam 'Abd al-'Aziz Imam Al-Sharif (better known as Abd al-Qadir ibn Abd Al-Aziz or by the moniker Dr. Fadl), former *mufti* of the Egyptian Islamic Jihad (EIJ) and mentor to Ayman al-Zawahiri, released a much anticipated work countering Al-Qa'ida's methods.[178] Dr. Fadl is considered by Egyptians as one of the most influential *Jihadi* thinkers alive, and his previous books are considered core *Jihadi* readings in the education of *Jihadists* worldwide. To openly counter *Jihadi* ideology by one of the most respected present-day *Jihadi* thinkers is a significant strategic opportunity that slipped by silently and unnoticed by Western leaders. A summary of his argument to counter his previous books and Al-Qa'ida's methods is as follows:

　　　　　- Dr. Fadl utilizes legal interpretations and clarifications to counter the *Jihadist* use of violence to overthrow Islamic governments. He argues that it is religiously unlawful to do so and is counterproductive.

　　　　　- Dr. Fadl states that the practice of calling others to Islam (*Da'wa*), is a safer, non-violent and religiously tolerable way to channel grievances against a regime.

　　　　　- He states that Muslims should pardon (*al-'afw*) the harmful actions of others, forgive (*al-safh*) one's enemies, shun (*ali'rad*) those who advocate un-Islamic behavior, and to remain patient (*al-aabr*) throughout the challenges that lie ahead.

- He argues that one must consider the potential damage of a violent act and determine if it outweighs the potential benefits. Since that violence will ultimately lead to death, destruction and further violence, he concludes terrorism can never be justified within *sharia,* therefore, must never be used while claiming religious precedence.

- Lastly, he highlights, using historical example, that after decades of political violence by *Jihadis* against the Egyptian government, no change in the entrenched regime occurred and the violence only resulted in fruitless casualties.[179]

Dr. Fadl's message is extremely powerful and could have been exploited by both moderate Islamic scholars as well as our own strategic communications apparatus. He is a legitimate former *Jihadi* who is credible amongst the Islamist activists, and his counter-argument to Al-Qa'ida's is significant. But Dr. Fadl is not alone, there are other former *Jihadis* who have "come out" recently against terrorism and the violent methods of Al-Qa'ida.

In the summer of 2004, two senior Islamic Jihad in Egypt (EIJ) members crafted a document called <u>Visualization</u> which rejected violent attempts to overthrow Islamic governments. Nabil Na'im, who assumed a senior leader role in EIJ after al-Zawahiri departed and a colleague Ismail Nasr, urged the Al-Azhar University scholars to publicly address and support their argument, but they failed to generate the support that was needed.[180] This was another missed opportunity by both moderate Muslim scholars and the West, to credibly counter *Jihadi* ideologies. Only by employing significant resources to monitor web sites, Arab news, web blogs, articles, and books, can we have any chance to seize upon any future coming-outs or arguments that directly counter and attack the Al-Qa'ida ideology and that of hard-line *Salafists*.

2) <u>Share in the Dialogue with Islamic Theologians</u>. Sheikh Mohammed Sayyed al-Tantawi, is the current Grand Imam of Al-Azhar Mosque and University, Cairo, Egypt. The Al-Azhar mosque and university are named in honor of Fatima Az-Zahraa, the daughter of the Prophet. Built circa 971 AD, Al-Azhar is believed to be the oldest mosque in the world and Muslim students attending the university study the *Qu'ran* and Islamic law in detail.[181] Recently, the Grand Imam addressed the ongoing issue in the post 9/11 world; the issue of a distorted image of Islam. He expressed the following:

> To rectify the image of Islam, larger numbers of scholars who specialize in religious affairs should be designated to explain to others in Europe and America the tolerant rulings of Islam, its noble laws, and sublime ethics while showing that the religion of Islam gives each person his due, fights terrorism, preserves the human soul, and considers the killing of one human being tantamount to the killing of all of humanity. Our duty in Al-Azhar is to show the whole world that Islam is against terrorism, murder, bloodshed, destruction and anything that leads to chaos and disorder in any society. The *Qu'ran* says that killing one human being is tantamount to the killing the whole of humanity and that saving the life of one human being is like saving the whole of humanity. We have to explain this to people in the East and West. This is what we have advised, demanded, and suggested to other preachers in the East and West. We tell them to explain the tolerance and mercy of Islam to people.[182]

His eminence, Grand Imam al-Tantawi's open denouncement of terrorism is indicative of what other Islamic experts also believe, but have yet to voice openly. Through our own Muslim communities and mosques, and those of nations with whom we partner with in fighting Al-Qa'ida, we should further develop a relationship with not only this Imam, his mosque and University, but others worldwide. A comprehensive approach of how we (the West) and Islamic nation can benefit from this relationship should be forwarded, discussed, and then pursued over time. The students who attend daily classes and lectures should be a target audience we indirectly attempt to influence through developing common perceptions and understandings with their religious leaders and most respected scholars.

3) <u>Divulge and Exploit Al-Qa'ida Marriages of Convenience</u>. Al-Qa'ida will likely attempt to enter into a marriage of convenience with other Islamic terrorist organizations whose ideologies may run counter to that of Al-Qa'ida and *Salafi-Jihadis*. The Egyptian extremist group, The Muslim Brotherhood (MB), is widely regarded as the original breeding ground for modern *Jihadi* terrorist groups. Hamas, the Islamic Resistance Movement of Palestine and Al-Qa'ida all evolved from the MB and subsequently, have similar ideological roots as well as modern day linkages with respect to *Sunni* Islamist extremism. Al-Qa'ida's growing relationship with Hamas is of special interest, because credible evidence exists Hamas has developed a strategic relationship or marriage of convenience, with Iran. In 2006, Khaled Mashaal, head of Hamas' Political Bureau declared in a Iranian news conference that "Iran's role with regards to Palestine should continue to increase," indicating Hamas was clearly prepared to open up Gaza to Iranian influence.[183] As the AQAM and its associated groups become more interconnected and grow, cross-pollination between *Jihadis* will eventually occur. Bin Laden is a pragmatist who will look to establish relationships with other zealots and across invisible lines of groups with differing ideologies or theologies, as well as partner with criminal elements for logistical purposes.

Experts have also identified the growing relationship between Al-Qa'ida and Hizbullah, the Iranian-backed *Shi'a* Islamic nationalist group fighting in Lebanon. Al-Zawahiri has previously made statements to bridge the sectarian divide, in which he acknowledges Hizbullah's legitimate Jihad against Israel and referred to them as brothers.[184] This "marriage" is tenuous at best and needs to be exploited, by using Al-Qa'ida's own ideology and words against them. Hassan Nasrallah, leader of Hizbullah has openly condemned bin Laden and Al-Qa'idas tactics and in the <u>Washington Post</u>, was quoted as labeling the Taliban as "The worst most dangerous thing that Islamic revival has encountered."[185] The potential friction and ideological differences can be exploited and Al-Qa'ida should be attacked on the grounds that they are not acting or growing relationships within their own ideology and relationships with *Shi'a* terrorist groups is inconsistent with the root principles of *Salafism*. An approach that would discredit bin Laden and al-Zawahiri and slowly erode future support from *Sunni* Muslims is to expose the marriage of convenience and inextricable linking both to *Shiite* movements and indirectly Iran, the more hated Persian *Shi'as*.

4) <u>Challenge the Jihadi and his Beliefs</u>. While we may not be able to eliminate all hard-line *Jihadis* prior to future attacks, we should attempt to shake the individual *Jihadi's* confidence in his beliefs and the cause. We do not have to necessarily convince them that their cause is wrong, but only sow doubt in their minds about the "justness" of the cause, and what could possibly happen to them and their families in the event Al-Qa'ida's promise of a martyr's journey after death is false.

5) <u>The Amman Message Opportunity</u>. On the eve of the 27th Ramadan 1425 AH, (November 9, 2004) in a religious sermon before King Abdullah Al-Hussein of Jordan, the Amman message was issued. The message and sermon was a call to re-emphasize Islam's core values of compassion, respect, unity across the Muslim world, acceptance, and freedom of religion.[186] In July 2005, King Abdullah and Jordon hosted an

international conference of two hundred of the world's most prominent Islamic scholars (*'Ulama*) from over fifty countries. The Islamic religious experts would issue a unanimous ruling and subsequent *fatwa* on three fundamental points:

- Specific recognition and validation of all eight Islamic legal schools (*Mathabs*) of *Sunni*, *Shi'a* and *Ibadhi* Islam; of traditional theology (*Ash'arism*); of Islamic mysticism (*Sufism*), and of true *Salafi* thought.

- *Takfir* was forbidden between Muslims.

- Subjective and objective preconditions were established for the issuing of *fatwas*, hereafter condemning illegitimate edicts in the name of Islam or Allah.[187]

One constant theme throughout the Amman ruling was that extremists were at fault for blackening the image of Islam and discrediting the Prophet, and that the extremists were to blame for the everyday Muslim people's fear of Western societies.[188]

The immediate significance of the Amman message is that it was intended to "put doubt in the minds" of *Jihadis* who trust the discourse of extremist clerics and scholars. During an interview, Jordon's King Abdullah reiterated that the reason for the Amman message was to remind the *Jihadis* that their spiritual leaders guidance and ideologies were against Islamic law.[189] The more significant outcome of the Amman message is the realization that under the recommendation of a respected Muslim regime leader, Islamic scholars collectively worked together to issue a unified message. Having a established an Islamic precedent, there exists future opportunities to influence and leverage this same body of respected Islamic authorities to issue additional *fatwas* that more clearly and explicitly denounce Al-Qa'ida and the use of terrorism in the name of Islam. *Fatwas* that must separate radical Islamists and label them political extremists who seek to destroy established order and legitimacy through subversion, intimidation, and terrorism.

There will be future prospective strategic opportunities that must be leveraged in order to further discredit Al-Qa'ida and *Salafi Jihadists* and to weaken their brand. We must be patient and deliberate in our long term approach, and quietly build relations with the Islamic scholars and leaders who are in the best position to issue *fatwas* and religious rulings. We might also be served well by identifying our own Muslim voices inside America and the West and look to co-opt them in a unified effort to credibly attack the *Jihadis* in the war of ideologies. We must wean ourselves off of trying to justify unpopular United States foreign policies in the Middle East, and go back on the offensive and influence Muslims of Al-Qa'ida's illegitimate ideology and negative actions that have served to hurt Islam and defile God.

Steal, Read, Understand, and Counter the Al-Qa'ida Playbook

In February 2006, the Combating Terrorism Center published "Stealing Al-Qa'ida's Playbook". Jarret Brachman and William McCants argue that the key to defeating the *Jihadi* movement is to identify and counter their strengths, exploit their vulnerabilities and to do so we must have the insight on where to look which is inside the *Jihadi* dialogue.[190] As both observed, *Jihadi* leaders tend to be extremely transparent, open, and blunt about their strengths and weaknesses. In order to recruit followers their beliefs and strategic vision are available through many mediums to include videos, audio recordings, and more extensively online through websites. A byproduct of the GWOTs focus on denying terrorists safe-haven and the destroying of several training and indoctrination camps in Afghanistan and Iraq, almost all of the *Jihad* ideology, training manuals, tactics and strategic observations are available online. In essence, Al-Qa'ida's playbooks are available for exploitation.[191]

One example to highlight is the writings of Abu Bakr Naji's, an influential *Jihadist* who has continued to rise in stature since the 9/11 attacks. Naji's expertise is evident in that he urges *Jihadis* to study Western diplomacy, military, management styles, economic trends, political theory, and sociology in order to identify the vulnerabilities. He himself has studied the United States and offers a coherent and plausible grand strategy to defeat us and how to exploit our vulnerabilities. Aside from offering his strategic vision, Naji also discloses the movement's vulnerabilities and weak points. Maintaining operational security, replacement of leaders and resolving chains of command, identifying spies, maintaining credibility for future recruits, and avoiding splintering along ideological lines are all very real issues, and all very exploitable.[192]

By dedicating the resources and training the proper individuals, we will continue to make greater headway in identifying core strengths and vulnerabilities of our terrorist adversaries. By all accounts the information is available both through unclassified online sites and also through intercepted messages and captured and exploited documents. Although Al-Qa'ida operates under a shroud of secrecy, they must make their vision and operational strategies known as well as their ideological underpinnings, in order to draw recruits and also support from charities, individuals, or states.

Examination of the Al-Qa'ida vast array of published literature and manuals and numerous statements points to an eight phase plan to wage a historic long-term war against the United States and our allies in the Middle East. A brief summarized account of the eight distinct phases are:

- I. <u>Awakening the Masses</u>. Expose Muslims to the threat of corrupt apostate regimes and American and Western hostility and moral bankruptcy. Enhance the image of *Salifism* as the only entity in the Arab world that is willing and capable to fight.

- II. *"Harb Istinzaf"* – <u>Long War of Attrition</u>. Bleed our enemies until they crumble. Bleed implying economically, militarily, and politically until America no longer holds the will to fight.

- III. <u>Sever Western/Muslim Alliances</u>. Cause the American withdrawal from the Middle East and subsequently sever alliances with secular and moderate regimes (Egypt, Jordon, Saudi Arabia, Pakistan etc). Without United States economic aid these countries will weaken and ultimately lose the support of their people.

- IV. *"Tasfiyat Hisabat"* – <u>Settling Old Scores</u>. Al-Qa'ida intends to overthrow the weakened regimes and "settle scores" by eliminating their leaders and security forces.

- V. *"Idarat al-Tawahush"* – <u>Management of Barbarism</u>. (Naji's influence). The most dangerous phase where Al-Qa'ida and its sympathizers will manage Arab and Muslim lands for a short period following the collapse of apostates. Chaos is expected due to the lack of security forces and the lawlessness that will follow.

- VI. <u>Establishment of *Shari'a* (Islamic Law)</u>. Pious religious governments will rise and rule Arab and Muslim states by *shari'a* for a temporary period, until the long awaited return of the caliphate.

- VII. <u>Remove all Western influence from the Middle East</u>. Full liberation of Muslim lands from the West to include the liberation of Palestine and subsequent destruction of the state of Israel. Retrieval of lands that were once Muslim owned, to include Spain and the Kashmir.

- VIII. <u>Reestablishment of the Caliphate</u>. Once all previous phases are achieved and following full liberation of all Muslim lands, the intent is to reestablish the caliphate and single entity rule for the entire Muslim community.[193]

If we are to believe the strategic path to the Caliphate highlighted above is fairly reliable then we can organize and orchestrate our own strategy and campaign plan to counter and deny Al-Qa'ida their ultimate goal. Regardless, the primary takeaway is that Al-Qa'ida will continue to publish their strategic and often their operational visions; all of which we can utilize and exploit.

Attack Al Qai'da Weaknesses and Vulnerabilities

As addressed previously, Al-Qai'da is not without identifiable vulnerabilities. Our best approach to tackling both strategic and operational vulnerabilities is to do so from multiple angles, using all instruments of national power and multinational resources that combines soft, hard, indirect and, at times, direct attacks. Listed below are some key vulnerabilities that should be considered for immediate exploitation and through the duration of the ILWCP.

1) <u>The al-Zarqawi Factor</u>. It is apparent that al-Zarqawi became a rogue element, with a singular agenda and that his allegiance to Al-Qa'ida and bin Laden was one of mutual convenience only. He overtly chastised scholars such as al-Zawahiri and al-Maqdisi, who he implied were not true *Jihadis* since they were away from the real fighting, unlike the operational and field commanders and *Jihadis* on the front lines in Iraq. Zarqawi's greatest operational error was following an exclusionary path (*takfir*) as

evidenced by his rejection of tribal affiliations, the *Shi'ites*, all Arab governments, and his ideological disagreements with the *Salafi* ideologues.[194] Although Al-Qa'ida in Iraq proved exceptionally adept at evolving and adapting, their brutal and arcane methods such as torture and beheadings, alienated more Muslims then motivated them to join his ranks. AQIZ was a true "franchise" of Al-Qa'ida and bin Laden, therefore we must make the logical argument amongst Islamists that bin Laden and the *shura* council condoned all methods and tactics, and hold them accountable. The ideological differences between Al-Qa'ida in Afghanistan and Iraq must be elevated in order to create internal dissension amongst the greater movement. Generating competition amongst the groups will lead to additional friction and impact the movements ability to coordinate larger scale operations.

The lessons from Al-Zarqawi's time as leader of AQIZ are numerous, but worthy of studying and integrating into our ILWCP. A future operational objective of pitting "franchises" against mother Al-Qaida in Afghanistan would have to be well developed and implemented through indirect and direct information operations. Labeling any influential Jihadi leader as *takfir*, can also be exploited along the lines that *takfirians* are incapable of accepting anything less then pure Islamic values. Although Abu Musab al-Zarqawi was a ruthless *Jihadi* his untimely end is telling and important. The message to others who want to be like him is that we will pursue you and use all necessary means to either kill or capture you, and you will never be safe.

2) <u>Recruits, Volunteers and Defectors</u>. Three key components of both our future Grand National Strategy and supporting campaign plan will focus on discouraging future recruits, demoralizing volunteers, and attracting potential defectors.

The most telling message that can be aimed directly at future recruits is that Al-Qa'ida sponsors murder and that they have killed more Muslims then all Western nations combined. Images of dead Islamic women and children are irrevocable evidence against what Islam stands for and scholars claim it to be. Islamists must have choices, and a moderate non-violent alternative is the path that can be shown is most likely to achieve the individual's goals. A large portion of Al-Qa'ida's *Jihadis* are recruited from mosques. Therefore, we must look to influence the most militant of clerics and either coerce, co-opt, or have them removed-neutralized, while offering more moderate clerics resources to provide for the education of their constituencies.

A similar strategy is required for the current bevy of volunteers and supporters of terrorist groups. These individuals are furthest from their leaders, but are still important to the greater movement. Injecting distrust from within, and infiltrating these ranks with operatives to gather intelligence and spread rumors, would increase the friction and slowly erode support from this faction. Terrorism must lose its appeal for this faction and become a very unattractive method of conflict. Targeting family members in order to use that leverage to work against volunteers is a reliable tactic, when feasible. They must see their radical leaders killed, captured, or watch them defect in order for them to comprehend that their only outcome is a bad one, if they continue with their support for *Jihad*. The case has been made that the Jihad these groups are waging, is in fact un-Islamic, and they must know if they seek martyrdom they will only disgrace their families and their God. Financiers must understand that their livelihood and the well-being of their families are at stake, and we must coerce them away from providing unlimited funding and resources to Al-Qa'ida and *Salafi-Jihadists*.

The *Chieu Hoi* (Open Arms) Program during the Vietnam War persuaded more

then 100,000 enemy Soldiers to defect to the South Vietnamese authorities. Individuals

were offered amnesty, given jobs, and or cash and, in many cases, integrated into allied

units as Kit Carson Scouts, operating in areas from where they had previously

operated.[195] As we fight using the ILWCP over an extended time period a generation of

Jihadis will tire and possibly become disaffected since they are unable to make

significant gains in the path toward the caliphate. Offering potential defectors a golden

bridge, to include amnesty would be a critical component of our strategy. Defections can

be easily exploited, and would further affect morale of those who choose to remain in

their organizations, while being discredited by those that are free from the grips of Al-

Qa'ida.

      3) <u>Deny Al-Qa'ida a relationship with the Islamic Nation *(Ummah).*</u> Al-Qa'ida is

not the defender of Islam, and Islam is not under siege by the United States. Al-Qa'ida

ideology and the followers of violent *Salafism* have twisted and rewritten sacred Islamic

canon for their own totalitarian desires. Al-Qa'ida recruits individuals for suicide attacks

and brands them martyrs, yet no senior Al-Qa'ida leader or ideologue has ever been a

martyr himself. Al-Qa'ida propagates an ideology of hatred and labels Christians, Jews,

Shi'ites, *Sufis*, and Hindus as unbelievers, yet the *Qu'ran* acknowledges all religions

and scholarly interpretation promotes freedom to choose your religion. Al-Qa'ida blames

others for the plight of the everyday Muslim, yet they have made no contributions

toward the building of civil services or quality of life improvements. These are just a few

messages that are factual in nature which could be used to amputate the linkage

between Al-Qa'ida and the *ummah*.

There are numerous other vulnerabilities and schisms within Al-Qa'ida and the movement, and more will present themselves over time. It is imperative we identify them and develop a fully integrated approach to widening any cracks in their foundation by countering their strengths and exploiting their weaknesses.

Targeting Priorities

Effective targeting requires credible and timely intelligence that is actionable. Unlike the Cold War days where the Central Intelligence Agency (CIA) enjoyed some success in the recruitment of KGB moles and persuasion of high ranking Soviet Officials to defect, the same approach has met with limited success in the current GWOT. Al-Qa'ida's core organization in Afghanistan and Pakistan has so far, proven impervious to damaging leaks or defections.[196] This is largely due to our Cold War approach of recruiting highly placed informants and our lack of culturally savvy and Arabic language speaking field agents. Not to mention that true hardcore Islamic extremists, willing to fly airplanes into buildings are rarely, if ever, motivated by money in the form of payoffs or bribes. It will take more time to grow human intelligence sourcing, that can complement our technological superiority in signals and imagery intelligence. Regardless, our Grand National Strategy must illustrate the appropriate target sets we intend to destroy, neutralize, or permanently influence. To be considered for current and future effects based planning and targeting:

1) <u>Counter Leader Targeting and Discrete Operations</u>. Certain radical extremist leaders and clerics must be eliminated. These individuals stand no chance of being converted, and the benefits of their deaths must outweigh the disadvantages. Al-Qa'ida is adept enough to replace any key leader, to include the *emir* bin Laden, but his

capture or death would significantly negatively impact the greater organization's morale. Bin laden has reached near mythical status amongst the *ummah* and his violent death, like al-Zarqaw'is, would serve to remind all *Jihadis* that no one, not even the *emir* is able to hide for ever. *Jihadis* must understand they only have three options: 1) die, 2) give up the cause, 3) defect. Achieving martyrdom status by their actions must be firmly countered through *Qu'ranic* interpretation by Islamic scholars. Al-Qai'da and AQAM key leaders must be identified tracked and targeted through a combination of kinetic and non-kinetic means.

Discrete Operations would be one important method to achieve a desired effect, while denying over excessive United States involvement. Small level Discrete Operations proved effective during the Philippines Counterinsurgency (1899-1902) as well as in Vietnam. During the Vietnam War, U.S. Special Forces trained indigenous tribesmen to conduct targeted killing operations against both Vietcong and North Vietnamese leaders.[197] Having a local face on the operatives would distance the United States in order to maintain legitimacy and to overtly deny involvement. For obvious reasons, much of this would have to be covert in nature and would take time, trainers, linguists, and resources to establish an initial operational capability as well as have some method of target approval and validation. Still, we have some historical precedent and a small success rate when applied and this could be an effective component in our growing arsenal of kinetic and non-kinetic methods against terrorists.

2) Phoenix *Partie Deux*. A significant component of the American counterinsurgency strategy in Vietnam from 1967 through 1972 was the Phoenix Program. Phoenix was a CIA run intelligence and security program designed and run by

the CIA in coordination with South Vietnam's legitimate security forces. Phoenix was designed to attack the covert Vietcong infrastructure (VCI) (estimated 100,000 operatives) living and working amongst the South Vietnamese society. The VCI conducted financing, performed recruiting for Vietcong and North Vietnamese units, political indoctrinations, human intelligence gathering, and some logistical support.[198] Over the five year period of the program's "official" existence, Phoenix was effective in neutralizing (through infiltration, killing and capture) the infrastructure that was directly supporting insurgency in South Vietnam.

U.S. Army Special Forces Officer Colonel Ken Tovo in his Army War College Strategic Research Project titled "From the Ashes of the Phoenix: Lessons for Contemporary Counterinsurgency Operations" skillfully highlights that the United States is currently facing an insurgency conducted by militant Islamic fundamentalist groups whose objectives are to overthrow legitimate regimes, reestablish an Islamic caliphate under *shar'ia,* and ultimately destroy Israel, and overthrow the United States. Colonel Tovo argues that by implementing a Phoenix like program now, we can effectively neutralize the militant Islamic infrastructure (MI2) that supports today's Islamic terrorist groups.[199]

Colonel Tovo makes a convincing argument and the strategic lessons of the Vietnam War should not be overlooked in fighting Al-Qa'ida and *Salafi-Jihadists.* Phoenix *Partie Deux* could be implemented to compliment our current ongoing counterinsurgency operations in Afghanistan, Iraq, the Philippines, and could be expanded to the HORN of Africa. Resourcing would come from Congressional funding, while manpower could be provided by the military and across the interagency (CIA,

Justice, Homeland Security, et cetera). However, unlike in Vietnam, a recommendation is not to utilize the CIA to run the program, but to create a combined interagency Task Force that would work directly for the Coalition Force Commander or COCOM Commander.

3) <u>High Value Targeting</u>. Combinations of both lethal and non-lethal means are required to directly attack the following high value target groups (listed in priority).

- <u>Leadership</u>. Leaders are hard to replace, even more so for iconic leaders like bin Laden, al-Zawahiri and al-Zarqawi. Kill, capture, co-opt, and discredit are all suitable tasks. Deter is acceptable but less likely to occur with high level leaders.

- <u>Command, Control and Communications Cells</u>. Discredit, destroy, disrupt, or neutralize are satisfactory tasks.

- <u>Networks</u>. Disrupt, discredit, sever, disinformation, destroy the networked linkages between Al-Qa'ida and the movement of aligned – networked terror cells and groups.

- <u>Facilitators (Financiers, Middlemen, Recruiters, Propaganda and Computer Experts)</u>. Dissuade, co-opt, seek defection, disinform, neutralize – counter, capture, and convert-turn tasks associated at members of this group. Converting facilitators to turn against their masters as well as neutralizing and countering effective Al-Qa'ida propaganda are critical desired effects.

- <u>Islamist activists</u>. Convincing this larger group to agree that Al-Qa'ida is a common enemy for both the West and the Islamic nation, thereby driving a wedge between Al-Qa'ida, *Salafi Jihadis* and their most reliable supporters.

- <u>Moderate Ideologues and Clerics</u>. Convince, co-opt, coerce, or partner with this critical group of Islamic scholars, in order to provide a moderate alternative to radicalism and to counter the extremists' rhetoric.

- *Ummah* (Muslim people). Influencing Muslims is the overriding task, with the desired effects of: 1) deterring future recruits for Islamist terror groups, 2) separate Islamist terrorist organizations from the *Ummah*, thereby reducing their popular support.

- <u>Criminal links</u>. Evidence is growing Al-Qa'ida and other *Salafi Jihadi* organizations are partnering with transnational criminal organizations, in order to move funding, resources, acquire WMD, or to move recruits into current conflict zones. Criminal organizations are normally not wedded to the radical ideologies of Islamist terrorist organizations and operate on the motive of profit. Targeting these groups can severely hinder AQAM's ability to conduct future attacks as well as sustaining current operations globally.

- <u>Arab and Islamic Media</u>. A critical effect to achieve is to have more fair and balanced reporting of both good and bad, from the operational front lines as well as through our strategic communications efforts. Influencing these groups is essential in order to *ReBrand* America.

- <u>Arab State and Muslim Senior Leaders (Jordon, Egypt, Saudi Arabia, Pakistan, Iraq, et cetera)</u>. Through public and private diplomacy we will need to influence the recognized leaders of several Islamic states in order to develop partnerships, share information – intelligence, increase counterterrorism capabilities and to also convince those regimes considered apostate by *Salafi-Jihadists*, to engage in true social reforms for their people.

- <u>Hizbullah, Hamas, and other non-*Salafi* Islamist Organizations</u>. Special focus must be paid to preventing alliances to develop between AQAM groups and non-*Salafi* motivated Islamist organizations, like Hamas and Hizbullah. The effect to achieve is to isolate Al-Qa'ida and deny them a greater larger network of partners. We should also work to create noticeable friction between these organizations (divide and conquer). To do so, we will have to enter into the dialogue with the groups and assume a *Realpolitik* approach (we are friends because my enemy is your enemy). Furthermore, any new alliances with Al-Qa'ida that could occur, will cause us to work diligently in order to expose and then destroy them, to prevent a greater global insurgency or Global Jihad from occurring.

      - <u>Terror Financing Organizations</u>. I will address this in further detail later in the paper.

Several other target groups exist but I believe these are currently the most significant in our development of an integrated approach to achieve desired effects using a mix of kinetic and non-kinetic means.

Thoughts on Funding, Schools, and Prisons

Terrorist organizations require funding, like oxygen, to survive. Funding available to Al-Qa'ida can come from a variety of means:

      - Oil Revenues

      - State sponsors (both directly, indirectly through third parties, and indirectly through the funding for radical mosques, *madrassas* et cetera)

      - Transnational Crime Organizations – (a mini global economy estimated at two trillion dollars)[200]

- Crime, Piracy, Drugs, and other illegal or black market activities

- Through Islamic NGOs and charities

- Individual personal wealth (e.g. Osama bin Laden)

- Money laundering

- Diversion of funds from legitimate international efforts (UN programs, WFO, humanitarian efforts etc.)

- Kidnapping and hostage ransoms

- Saudi Arabian *sharia* investment banks

The challenge of tracking the intricate networks of terrorist financing is that they are extremely sophisticated, well-developed, entrenched, and is often hidden amongst legitimate organizations. Bin Laden, expertly leveraged the Islamic principle of *zakat*, (one of the five pillars of Islam), to raise finances for the *Jihad* against the Soviets in Afghanistan. Utilizing fundraisers in Afghanistan, Riyadh, and Washington, it is estimated he collected over $3.5 billion U.S. dollars to fund the *mujahidin* – Afghani fighters during the war.[201] Additionally, another lesson learned by Al-Qa'ida from the Bosnian War, was to funnel finances through Islamic charitable and humanitarian organizations, to hide the movement of significant amounts of funds.

Since the 9/11 attacks more then one hundred countries implemented terrorism legislation or regulations, including laws to block money-laundering, the misuse of Islamic charities, and funding for terrorist organizations.[202] Over the past seven years the United States has led a multi-national effort to identify, track, and seize terrorist related funds. The United States has had some success by using our own Anti-Terrorism and Effective Death Penalty Act of 1996, which allows for the freezing of suspected terrorist group assets within the United States, thereby making it a criminal offense for Americans to provide funding and other forms of material support.[203] But more targeted laws, international cooperation, and enhanced powers are required in order to make a larger more significant impact on the current methods of terror financing.

An emerging issue that cannot be overlooked and that we must develop a course of action to pursue against is the Saudi financial practices. In her book, Funding Evil: How Terrorism is Financed and How to Stop It, Dr. Rachel Ehrenfeld argues that certain Saudi Arabian individuals are subversively funding terrorism with the goal of defeating the United States through economic warfare. She outlines the concept of shari'a financing (meaning abide by Islamic Laws), which is a byproduct of the twentieth century and invented by the Egyptian Muslim Brotherhood. Dr. Ehrenfeld provides a detailed account of how Saudi Arabian shari'a banks are investing massive amounts of funds (estimated $800 Billion to $1 trillion U.S. Dollars) for investment worldwide in order to cripple the West economically.[204] Saudi's are using money in order to corrupt the West, fund terrorism, and eventually take over the West through shari'a compliant investments.[205] She claims that Saudi banks currently own over twenty percent of the New York Stock Exchange and forty-six percent of the London Stock Exchange, while continuing to buy more.[206] Without a well thought-out approach and hard evidence, we will have limited ability to deter this current practice by the Saudi's which is clearly undermining our national security and possibly threatens our future.

Moreover, it is estimated today that Saudi Arabia has funneled at a minimum $70 billion U.S. dollars worldwide to spread Wahhabism and fundamentalist ideology by financing hundreds of radical mosques and extremist clerics, *madrassas* and Islamic centers.[207] This funding is directed at increasing anti-Western sentiment as well as setting the conditions for future terrorist recruitment while supporting ongoing operations.

As the dollar continues to weaken and the petro-dollar strengthens, we must develop counter-strategies to the emerging economic problems. Formalizing international partnerships to introduce necessary international conventions and treaties, and capacity building to identify, track, and then target illicit terrorist funding is a necessity. As importantly, a strategy of what to do with respect to Saudi Arabia's indirect financial actions must be vetted and implemented with strong conviction.

Equally troubling is the findings in a 2006 report entitled, <u>Saudi Arabia's Curriculum of Intolerance</u>, by the Freedom House's Center for Religious Freedom and Cooperation. After careful review of numerous Saudi Ministry of Education textbooks, the organization summarily agreed that a theme of religious intolerance toward other religions, as well as a central focus on *Wahhabism* as the only true form of Islam, was noted throughout. More specifically the major prolific themes are:

- Condemned and denigrated all other Muslims who do not follow the *Wahhabi* sect of *Sunni* Islam, calling them deviants. (Included are *Shi'a* and *Sufi* Muslims).

- Commands Muslims to "hate" Christians, Jews, non-*Wahhabi Sunnis*, other "unbelievers" and to treat them unjustly.

- Professes that Jews and Christians are true enemies of Islam and that there exists a perpetual class between civilizations.

- Forwards conspiracy theories by accusing Freemasons, Lions Clubs and Rotary Clubs of plotting to undermine Muslims.

- Asserts that the spread of Islam through *Jihad* is a religious duty. Fighting between Muslims and Jews must continue until judgment day, until Muslims receive their promised victory.[208]

Saudi Ministry officials continue to claim they are reforming their textbooks and have made positive steps toward a more tolerant approach. But, until hard evidence is provided, we can continue to expect that the next generation of Saudi educated children will grow up to be adults with a significant bias against all other religions as well as non-*Wahhabi* sects. The significance of this being that Saudi Arabs will continue to be fertile grounds for terrorist recruitment in the future.

Another breeding ground for Islamist activists and terror groups are prisons, both inside the United States and worldwide. Extremists have been known to infiltrate prison religious programs, and pollute their audience with fundamentalist literature, as well as *Wahhabi* doctrine.[209] We must also consider the possibility of foreign sponsored infiltration of U.S. prisons, with the goal of developing homeland terror cells. The United States has a history of Islamic militants breeding out of prisons with the Weathermen, Weather Underground, Black Panthers, and Black Liberation Army emerging on the scene in the late 1960s early 1970s.[210] Additional information in this specific area must be collected and can be achieved through the use of well-placed infiltrators or the coercion of current prison personnel that are under incarceration in our prisons.

Several opportunities are available to work with moderate Islamic clerics and scholars as well as indirectly providing resources to moderate Islamic activist movements that do not promote terror and violent *Jihad*. Prompting mainstream clerics to issue *fatwas* quickly after iconic terror attacks can only be done if we have developed those relationships over time. Influencing the Islamic clerics and scholars through soft approaches and on a theological basis would best serve our future leaders during engagements with these same influential Islamic figureheads. Engagements will be necessary in our overhaul of our strategic communications and public diplomacy.

Strategic Communications and Fighting in the 21st Century Information Environment

In support of our Grand National Strategy, we will need a well thought-out, tailorable, comprehensive, and nested strategy to diminish the appeal of radical Islamist group themes and to counter their messages. We have to develop a sophisticated communications strategy that can target local, regional, global, and other specific audiences, at times all in the same message. Words mean something and the words of our leaders from strategic through tactical levels, must be credible, truthful, and intended to influence.

1) <u>Strategic Themes</u>. Specific themes must be developed in concert with our grand strategy and ILWCP effort, and evolve over time as events occur, opportunities arise, and conditions change. A select few general themes to stimulate further development are:

- The West and democracy are not in conflict nor do they threaten Islam. We recognize Islam as a religion of peace and hope.

- American stands for the values of freedom, hope, justice, opportunity, and respect and human dignity for every individual.

- America and Islam have many common interests and common core values. Neither America nor the West is at war with Islam.

- Radical Extremists and extremist ideologies are the common enemy of all Muslims, Christians, Jews, Hindus, and all others who subscribe to peace and good will.

2) <u>Strategic Messages</u>. There are many and more will be needed as events occur and we engage our multiple audiences over time. Two important points that should be highlighted:

- The Message after the next massive terror attack. Having the benefit of hindsight, we should wargame and develop a package of communiqués, themes, and messages in the event we experience another 9/11 synchronized attack, or weapons of mass destruction are used against the United States homeland, our overseas interests, or our deployed military forces. The first hour to forty-eight hours are extremely critical after an epic attack and we must be perceived by multiple audiences as firmly in control of the situation, united, and fearless. We may have to co-opt our own major media outlets to achieve our desired effects in the name of national security.

- The wrong message at this critical juncture in the GWOT and in combating terrorist organizations is to continue to forcibly promote and push the "Democracy and Freedom Agendas." To not delete this from our strategic communications with our Islamic audiences will further prevent us from being able to effectively wage the war of ideas. When Muslims finally accept that Al-Qa'ida is **NOT** conducting a Holy War and, is instead, waging a campaign of murder against humanity, then we will begin to see credible gains in the war of ideas through our strategic communications efforts.

3) <u>Audiences</u>. Several audiences will continue to be targeted through use of strategic communications as well as identifying key influencers or opinion leaders (those whose views will have a ripple effect through and to a larger audience) and select individuals empowered by their position, who normally speak with authority.[211]

4) <u>Consistency and Patience</u>. Our messages must "stick," therefore, they must be heard through multiple means, multiple times, and remain relatively consistent over time. A gradual long-term approach to public diplomacy that is patient, demonstrably maintains or increases our credibility, is the goal. The message must "stick," and resonate.

5) <u>Waging Political Warfare</u>. A key component of combating transnational and state sponsored terrorist organizations is Political Warfare. Political Warfare is best defined as an art or the art of waging and winning a conflict by non-military means.[212] Our agenda must focus on attacking our enemy, beating him ideologically, keeping him in the wrong and then, while continuing to influence and convince both Islamists and non-Islamists that Islamist terrorists, threaten all religions and all humanity. We must appreciate that we are attempting to win over a very hostile and untrusting audience (Middle Eastern Muslims) from the hard core radicals. If we are to have any chance of success, our deeds will have to far exceed our words, or in other words *"Our video must exceed our audio!"* We will have significant opportunities over the duration of the campaign plan to slowly breakthrough the anti-Americanism sentiment that is currently on the rise in the Middle East as well as globally.

6) <u>Immediate or Short-Term Communications Objectives</u>.

- Engage in dialogue as opposed to monologue with the Islamic community.

- Identify and then resolve misunderstandings.

- Build and maintain relationships. Work toward a common purpose.

- Identify and discuss the common enemy (Al-Qa'ida, AQAM, *Salafi-Jihadists*, Islamist Terrorists).

- *Brand* the enemy leadership (desired response is negative).

- Attack that enemy's image, discredit, and take control of the dialogue. Counter their messages and discredit their acts, themes, and ideology.[213]

- *ReBrand* America (desired response is positive). Dispel caustic myths about our society while emphasizing we are a tolerant pluralistic society that embraces people of all religions. Highlight how American Muslims are not repressed and are fully integrated into our society of equals.

7) <u>Means to Communicate and Wage Political War</u>. Ayman al-Zawahiri was first to grasp the significance of the media and the importance of information domains. In July 2005, he released the following statement:

> We are in a battle, and more than half of this battle is taking place in the battlefield of the media..... we are in a media battle for the hearts and minds of the *umma*.[214]

We must balance our methods by developing themes and messages that can be communicated by direct means, indirect, or third party means, through key influencers, or as required by covert means. A few options for further development and refinement are:

121

- Buy and sponsor airtime and satellite TV stations that can reach the Middle East, Europe, and other Islamic places. Partner with a Muslim state or regional security entity to develop an alternative to *Al-Jazeera* and *Al-Arabia*.

- Fight terror on the Web. Create moderate Islamist sites, conduct discrediting operations on known Jihadi web sites, challenge AQAM statements using ideology and facts. Significant resources and technological and cultural as well as Islamic religious expertise will be required. Tomorrows *Jihadi* ideologues are blogging today on Al-Qa'ida web sites.

- Cyber-terrorism. Develop offensive as well as defensive capabilities.

- Defame and criticize senior *Jihadi* leaders by attacking from multiple fronts (cartoons, News, blogs, Web posts, television, radio broadcasts, et cetera). They live in a cave, or if not, have limited freedom to maneuver so our ability to stay inside their propaganda and information decision cycle is critical.

- Partner in the development of television shows that can reach the *ummah*. Shows can vary from Islamic Soaps, Security Force Reality TV, home improvement, world culture, and religious educational shows. If available through satellite technology, then transnational actors and corrupt regimes will have limited little capability to censor these shows.

- Over time, build a relationship with the current major and minor Islamic media outlets. Consistency and credibility are vital as we can reach multiple audiences who already tune-in to these networks.

- Degrade Al-Qa'ida information operations capabilities. In Afghanistan, printing presses are critical components, while worldwide strategic communication is passed via the Internet.

The 2007 United States National Strategy for Public Diplomacy and Strategic Communications is a significant positive step forward in gathering the entire interagency onto the same playing field. An update should be developed in conjunction with the development of a Grand National Strategy to Combat Islamist Terrorism that considers the recommendations that have been put forth in this strategic research project.

United States – Multifaceted Leader in the World.

The threat of terrorism is unlikely to lessen in the near-term. If we continue to focus solely on fighting tactical aspects of Al-Qa'ida, then victory and achievement of our strategic objectives will never be reached. We must assume an outlook that can see beyond our current counterterrorism efforts and radical *Salafi Islamism* threat to our way of life and global security. Five significant areas will now be addressed:

1) Champion other Causes. The United States must continue to not only champion counterterrorism efforts globally, but should also endeavor to take the lead in other causes such as: 1) the prevention of human suffering, 2) Natural Disaster Response – a Global capability, 3) become champions of international law, and 4) demonstrate genuine concern over global warming and world health issues to include HIV-Aids – pandemic flu and water shortage issues. Significant progress in a variety of these areas would go a long way toward diminishing the negative hegemonic hyper-power stereotype that we currently have. All of these efforts are costly, but arguably the second and third order benefits far outweigh the current short term financial burden.

2) <u>Arab History and the West</u>. The first confrontation between the Arab world and the West was in 1798, when Napoleon and the French invaded Egypt and swiftly and effortlessly conquered them. Arabs awoke to a new reality, one where Europe was a immensely powerful behemoth that not only threatened to steal their precious resources, but threatened the existence of civilization as they had come to know it.[215] Over the next two centuries, Arabs would continue to perceive that Western colonization was responsible for diseases, stagnation, and all other grievances. Anti-Western sentiment was prominent in several Arab societies well before Al-Qa'ida arrived on the scene. Nevertheless, the bin Laden-led Al-Qa'ida propaganda franchise has proven to be expert at furthering this perception amongst Muslims and also, for holding the United States accountable for the multitude of modern day problems that the everyday disaffected Muslim experiences.

3) <u>Western Perceptions</u>. The Western perspective of Arab governments is that leaders are more interested in regime control than they are about the lack of civil liberties, escalating unemployment, lawlessness, persistently stagnant economies, corruption and good governance.[216] Extremism may be a byproduct of weak, uncaring, or failing Islamic secular governments. We must put forward a strong agenda to push for societal, economic and civil reforms in those countries that terrorists are breeding from (Saudi Arabia, Syria, Libya, et cetera). A delicate balance of coercement, economic enticement with the allure of mutual beneficial gains both financially and diplomatically must underwrite these initiatives. Allowing for greater political participation by select *Jihadi* groups, groups that currently or have previously threatened secular governments (Muslim Brotherhood – Egypt, the *Shi'a* Again – Saudi Arabia), would be a

significant step towards serious political reforms.[217] Allowing Islamist activists an active voice and the ability to influence policy would significantly undercut the Al-Qa'ida strategy.

4) The Saudi Arabian Issue. The relationship between the United States and Saudi Arabia must change in light of the facts that indicate they may be indirectly waging a war of attrition against the economies of the West while simultaneously setting the conditions for the next generation of *Jihadis*. A much more detailed in-depth analysis must occur by a team of experts to include at a minimum, sociologists, economists, religious scholars, political scientists, and academicians. At this time, it is not prudent to recommend a specific strategy or policy changes for our relationship with Saudi Arabia, until the findings of such a study are made available. As we develop a strategy towards Saudi Arabia we must also look to renew the agenda with respect to Israel and Palestine.

5) Israel and Palestine. Since the end of hostilities of the Second World War, the issue of Palestine has continued to fester and serve as a greater source of conflict in the Middle East. A new road map for peace is one of the more compelling global issues today and one that terrorists have continually exploited to their benefit. Bin Laden and al-Zawahiri have over-magnified the United States' diplomatic and financial support to Israel, in order to increase anti-American sentiment and to further their cause. The perceived indifference of the United States Government of the plight of the Palestinians is and will continue to be a catalyst and motivator for recruitment and violent *Jihad*. The United States should assume the lead role in partnership with the international community, Arab states, and Israel to broker a long-term settlement or trusteeship. The

2007 Annapolis Conference, hosted by President Bush, was one small, but very positive step forward toward a peaceful settlement and resolution of the Palestinian issue. In the event an agreeable settlement is achieved within the next decade, removing the Palestine-Israel issue from the table will not solve the larger problems prevalent in the region. The only option that Al-Qa'ida will accept is total destruction of the Jewish state. Still, a negotiated settlement agreeable and enforceable by all parties involved would do much to undercut the Al-Qa'ida agenda and their legitimacy amongst the Arabs.

6) Multinational Counterterrorism. The U.S. will continue to lead and pursue a multinational approach to counterterrorism. Expanding our existing global counterterrorism network and sustaining our current allies in fighting terror is instrumental. Intelligence and information sharing has clearly improved as evidenced by numerous successful operations that have thwarted attacks on the homeland. We must seek to implement additional Bilateral, Multilateral, Regional, and International agreements (Security Cooperation, Inter-agency cooperation, military combined/joint activities, intelligence and information sharing, financial tracking, and confidence and security-building measures), building upon our current capabilities. Aligning incentives for Arab and Muslim states to combat Islamist terrorist organizations is a necessity. Perhaps through economic initiatives, we can develop mutually benefiting partnerships that provide additional income and jobs to the *ummah*, as opposed to the elites.

Violent extremist *Islamism* grew out of ignorance and dominance in the greater Middle East. The world community must recognize that Al-Qa'ida and its network of *Islamist* terrorist organizations represent a new age of terror as they strive to become apocalyptic change agents. Agents of fortune that desire to acquire and then use a chemical, biological, radiological, or nuclear explosive (CBRNE) weapon(s) of mass destruction – effects against the West.

7) <u>Global Commitment to Non-proliferation and use of WMD/WME</u>. The proliferation and use of Chemical, Biological, Radiological, and Nuclear Explosives by Al-Qa'ida must be universally agreed upon and enforced. Transnational, regional, and local terrorist groups must clearly understand that any proliferation or usage or of WMD/WME will meet with harsh-response from a full array of instruments of national power. We need to bring the Arab states into this coalition and leverage them, or coerce them if needed.

8) <u>Afghanistan – Pakistan</u>. The Government of Pakistan is continually exposed to a multitude of internal and external security challenges. The U.S. is partially to blame for the situation because of our unspecified policy objectives after the defeat of the Soviet Union at the hands of the *mujahidin*. Without any specified strategy or a desire to see a stable post-Soviet occupied Afghanistan, the conditions were inadvertently set for the growth of radical extremists. Al-Qa'ida and the Taliban were forged out of the Soviet-Afghan War, which takes us to present day and the current situation in the region.

Today, Pakistan is undeniably one of our essential partners in the war on terrorists. Recently, the Deputy Secretary of State, John Negroponte made these remarks before the Senate Foreign Relations Committee:

> Pakistan has been indispensable to our world-wide struggle against violent extremists, and successful American engagement with a stable and democratic Pakistan is vital to our national security interests. As Afghanistan's neighbor, Pakistan plays a pivotal role in the Coalition's war effort there. Without security and stability on the Pakistani side of the border, success in Afghanistan will prove elusive. Pakistan's future will also be decisive in the search for stability in South Asia – a region of vastly increased importance to the United States. The United States and

Pakistan have a common interest in the success of a robust and multi-faceted fight against violent extremism, focused on democracy and economic development as well as on security cooperation. We intend to pursue that common interest vigorously with Pakistan's next government[218]

Building Pakistan's counterterrorism expertise and developing additional economic opportunities that will ultimately benefit their growing middle class are two achievable goals. As a Muslim country taking the lead in the fight against Al-Qa'ida it can be leveraged towards greater commitments of other Muslim states.

9) <u>Building Relations with the Islamic Change Agents</u>. Egypt's Muslim Brotherhood, Palestine's Hamas, and Lebanon's Hizbullah, all began as Islamist activist organizations that ultimately reverted to the use of terror tactics as a means to achieve their stated political objectives. In 2006, Hamas was elected as the Parliament of the Palestinian Authority (responsible for governing Gaza and the West Bank). In June 2007, the Battle for Gaza erupted between Hamas and their rival political party Fatah who refused to handover the government.[219] Eventually hostilities ceased, and Fatah remained in power.

An opportunity may be presenting itself with the lawful election win by Hamas. Had they been able to actually assume control of the Palestinian Authority Parliament, could this have been the moment in time to initiate and open a dialogue with Hamas in an attempt to convince them to take steps away from guerilla warfare or attacks on Israeli Soldiers, and for them to condemn Islamist terror organizations such as Al-Qa'ida. Hizbullah has continued to move more to the middle in their actions and we should reassess our position on whether to open communications with this organization. One possible future is to work with these former terrorist organizations to pursue a non-violent agenda, and ultimately evolve away from the Islamist terrorism club.

We should constantly assess the global environment to determine if there are points in time to enter into the dialogue either directly or indirectly through third parties, Islamist terrorist organizations that can be influenced to denounce and discredit Al-Qa'ida. Of course this will have to be carefully executed and well thought-out, and not perceived by our Allies as the U.S. abandoning them. The point to press home is that organizations like Fatah, Hamas, and Hizbullah should strive through non-violent actions to push their political agendas, instead of reverting to terrorism. There may be future opportunities for the United States to shape and set conditions for this to occur in Muslim countries such as Egypt, Saudi Arabia, and Palestine as well.

Use of Military Force

The military will continue to play a pivotal role in our Grand National Strategy for counterterrorism and throughout the duration of the ILWCP. However, we should immediately reduce the signature and our forward military presence in the Middle East and continue to reduce presence, as the situation in Iraq becomes more stable. We have embraced an expeditionary mindset and can swiftly deploy, and seize the initiative and conduct decisive operations against any foe. Nevertheless, the types of battles we will likely fight during the campaign plan will be irregular, against asymmetric threats, and against forces who are knowledgeable and adept at fighting 4GW or possibly even 5GW. Developing Joint Doctrine with supporting Service Doctrine is required if we are to improve and expand our Irregular Warfare (IW) capabilities.

Knowing we currently have no near peer competitor today, nor will we in the next two decades, we would be better served if we slightly retailored a portion of our landpower towards counterinsurgency (COIN) and IW. We can assume that we will deploy forces in the future to conduct either necessary proxy wars or to assist legitimate government security forces with COIN expertise and IW capabilities. As mentioned previously standing up a revised Phoenix Program would provide an integral capability when conducting COIN. Enhancing our special operations forces with foreign internal defense – irregular warfare trained conventional landpower, would provide the United States greater capability to engage and conduct mil – mil partnerships, during Phase 0 conditions and through theater security engagement plans.

At all costs we must work diligently to avoid another major combat action in the Middle East at a minimum, for the remainder of the twenty-first century, if at all possible. Iran with their hegemonic intentions and aspirations of a nuclear weapons program is the current wild card that poses a significant threat and could eventually ignite another major combat operation in the region. One possible scenario is that the United States would be compelled to execute a preemptive decisive combat action in the event they acquire or intend to use WMD/WME, or can be proven to have supplied a transnational terrorist group with that capability. A combination of highly mobile and lethal BCTs, with sufficient Airpower, ISR and C4 could easily destroy the Iranian ground and air forces or pound them into submission, while the U.S. Navy could easily destroy Iranian naval forces while maintaining the sea lines of communication open for safe passage of commercial and military shipping. Phase IV after major combat operations in Iran, would take a significantly larger force to ensure security is maintained and stability and reconstruction operations could begin in earnest. The instability that would follow major combat operations is the fertile breeding ground that Al-Qa'ida seeks, in order to grow roots and infect others with their cancer.

One key to staving off a major war with Iran is to facilitate and set the conditions for a balance of power within the region amongst those states that reside in the region. Our theater security cooperation plans (TSCP) must be robust as well as our intelligence and information sharing agreements. Counterterrorism training would be a key component of our TSCP as well as border security, policing, criminal investigation, and legal training; all executed by a fully rounded-out interagency task force or team.

When fighting Al-Qa'ida's cells and fighters who are a part of an ongoing insurgency, utilizing the full complement of human intelligence, ISR, and strategic special operations as well as highly trained conventional forces is required. At the tactical level, we fight to kill or capture and destroy cells, but units are also working diligently to improve security and overall general public services, therefore, it takes a combined effort between the military and interagency to win.

The use of military force for major combat operations should always remain an option, but not the first option when considering solutions to emerging problems that pose a direct or indirect threat to our national security. But in order to have any chance of winning against the Al-Qa'ida movement we need a full commitment by our leaders, our government and its many entities, our international partners, our citizens, and the military to see the task through to completion.

War in the 22nd Century and Al-Qa'ida After Next

It can be guaranteed that war in the 21st century will continue to be brutal, violent, and good men and women will continue to die. Technological advancements in weaponry and network-centric capabilities will play a more significant role in our future major combat operations, but warfare will always entail chaos, uncertainty, and opportunity. Terrorism will still remain a viable tactic in the future, specifically for those ideologically motivated groups who cannot resource a standing or guerilla army, nor choose to enter into major combat operations.

Al-Qai'da is likened to a mythical serpent in the garden; symbolic of deceit and identified as a guardian of religion or sacred things. Al-Qa'ida will continue to envision itself as the guardian and vanguard for Islam, and we will experience more of its "fork-tongued" dialogue in the years ahead. The serpent will continue to hide inside the garden from prying eyes, using its natural surroundings to camouflage its movements as well as shedding its skin to signify its evolution, until a moment of its choosing where it can strike violently, causing death. The attacks on our embassies in Africa, upon the USS Cole, and on American soil on 9/11, are eerie reminders of how evil, vengeful, and unforgiving this hatred-inspired group of extremists truly is.

America and the West have lived for decades in a world that legally recognizes war. We subscribe to certain rules in war. Rules that protect non-combatants and innocents and that limit collateral damage and senseless loss of life, whenever operationally feasible and practical. We recruit, train, and then deploy Warrior-Statesman who operate under a code of conduct that is built upon ethical behaviors, and then when absolutely necessary, they kill. Al-Qa'ida inspired terrorists terrorize, kill, and murder because their leaders have twisted their ideology and have reshaped the true meanings of the sacred canon of Islam, the *Holy Qu'ran*. The paradox of their dilemma is that terrorism may, over time, achieve local tactical victories, but historically no terrorist organization has won and achieved its long term goals.[220]

Upon the violent death, or capture, or death by natural causes of Osama bin Laden, Al-Qa'ida will continue to reinvent itself with either a new generation of malevolent leadership or possibly fraction as members splinter off to form new offshoots of mother Al-Qa'ida. A resounding message that the hardcore Al-Qa'ida terrorists must always remember is the fact that they will either die violently, get captured, but rarely (Never) will they be allowed to retire and enjoy the fruits of their efforts. Offering them a golden bridge and a chance to quit and renounce their evil ways is a plausible option that we should pursue as this generation of Al-Qa'ida survivors grows weary of the struggle that they cannot and will not win.

Conclusion.

The Islamic world has for hundreds of years been one of turmoil and conflict, with its constituents psychologically battered and often disillusioned. Many governments and elitist rulers in the Middle East, fail terribly at providing the basic needs: food, clean water, energy, employment, and medical support to their populace. True changes at all levels, ruler to ruled, must occur in the region if there is any chance of harmony or peace. A "Winning Hearts and Minds Campaign" in the Middle East is an endeavor of several generations, that requires nearly unlimited resources, in order to earn the trust or overcome the suspicions that Muslims have of the West. A tall prospect, when those same critical resources are needed at home for domestic programs or in other critical hotspots around the world. For Al-Qa'ida and the *Salafi-Jihadis* to have been immutably defeated, their ideology will have had to been proven false, illicit, and in direct contradiction to the *Qu'ran* and *Sunnah*, and more importantly Muslims will have had to abandon their support to the *Salafi-Jihadi* terrorist organizations. If we and our international partners and Middle Eastern allies are to have any chance of winning, we will have had to orient the war through development of a Grand National Strategy and executed this war through an integrated long war campaign plan.

The purpose of this research project was to argue the case that Al-Qa'ida, its associated movement (AQAM) and *Salafi Jihadi* Islamist terrorists are our correct enemies, and that the United States will need to overhaul and rethink its long term strategy, objectives, and capabilities to defeat these terrorist organizations. I argued that our current National and Military Strategies to combat terrorism have served us well but are inadequate to wage a protracted war upon an ideological emboldened transnational foe, and that we would be better served by preparing ourselves to fight a war of several generations (long war) against these enemies. I then made several recommendations to include the development of a coherent Grand National Strategy for Terrorism and a supporting Integrated Long War Campaign Plan to execute the strategy. Al-Qa'ida, the Al-Qa'ida Associated Movement, and *Salafi-Jihadi* Islamist terrorists pose a direct threat to our national security and to the homeland, and only through the execution of a terrorism focused Grand National Strategy and ILWCP and by the synchronization of diplomatic, informational, military, and economic instruments of national power by an unified interagency effort in partnership with our multinational partners, international governmental and non-governmental organizations, and regional security organizations, can we achieve victory by our terms.

Endnotes

[1] U.S. Department of State, *A Strategic Assessment of Progress Against the Terrorist Threat*, eJournal USA Online, April 2007 (journal on-line); available from http://usinfo.state.gov/journals/itps/0507/ijpe/assessment.htm; Internet; accessed on 20 March 2008.

[2] U.S. National Intelligence Council, National Intelligence Estimate, *The Terrorist Threat to the US Homeland*, (July 2007), ps. 3-4.

[3] James M. Lutz and Brenda J. Lutz, *Global Terrorism,* (London and New York: Routledge, 2004), 8.

[4] Ibid., 10.

[5] Bruce Hoffman, "A Form of Psychological Warfare," eJournal USA Online, May 2007, (journal on-line), available from http://usinfo.state.gov/journals/itps/0507/ijpe/hoffman.htm; Internet; accessed on 21 March 2008.

[6] James J.F. Forest, "Preface," in *Terrorism and Political Islam: Origins, Ideologies and Methods – A Counterterrorism Textbook for the New Agent Training Program at the FBI Academy, Quantico, Virginia*, ed. James J.F. Forest (West Point, NY: Combating Terrorism Center, January 2007), ix.

[7] Hoffman, "A Form of Psychological Warfare", 2.

[8] Ibid., 2.

[9] David C. Rapoport, "The Four Waves of Rebel Terror and September 11," in *Terrorism and Political Islam: Origins, Ideologies and Methods – A Counterterrorism Textbook for the New Agent Training Program at the FBI Academy, Quantico, Virginia*, ed. James J.F. Forest (West Point, NY: Combating Terrorism Center, January 2007), 18 - 19.

[10] Ibid., p21.

[11] James Adams, *The Financing of Terror* (New York: Simon and Schuster, 1986) , 192.

[12] Brian Michael Jenkins, "The New Age of Terrorism," in *Terrorism and Political Islam: Origins, Ideologies and Methods – A Counterterrorism Textbook for the New Agent Training Program at the FBI Academy, Quantico, Virginia*, ed. James J.F. Forest (West Point, NY: Combating Terrorism Center, January 2007), 25.

[13] European Union, *Terrorism Situation and Trend Report 2007*, TE-SAT, European Terrorist Working Party, (The Hague, Netherlands: Europol, March 2007), 3 – 4.

[14] James J.F. Forest ed., *Teaching Terror: Strategic and Tactical Learning in the Terrorist World*, (Lanham, Maryland: Rowman and Littlefield, 2006), xi.

[15] Paul Pillar, *Terrorism and Foreign Policy* (Washington, D.C.: Brookings Institution Press, 2001), 47.

[16] Mohammed M. Hafez, *Suicide Bombers in Iraq: The Strategy and Ideology of Martyrdom*, (Washington, D.C.: United States Institute of Peace, 2007), 232 – 233.

[17] Brian Michael Jenkins, "The New Age of Terrorism", 31.

[18] Rohan Gunaratna, *Inside Al Qaeda: Global Network of Terror* (New York: Berkley Books, 2002), 1.

[19] Ibid., 4.

[20] Ibid., 5-6.

[21] Peter L. Bergen, *The Osama Bin Laden I Know: An Oral History of Al Qaeda's Leader* (New York: Free Press, 2006), 74-75.

[22] William McCants, ed. and Project Director, *Militant Ideology Atlas: Executive Report* (West Point, NY: Combating Terrorism Center, November, 2006), 5.

[23] Dr. Larry Goodson, "Middle East and Islam" lecture, U.S. Army War College Middle East Elective, Carlisle Barracks, PA, 26 March 2008, cited with permission of Dr. Goodson.

[24] McCants, *Militant ideology Atlas*, 5-6.

[25] Ibid., 6.

[26] Ibid.

[27] Abu Muhammad Asem al-Maqdisi, Wikipedia Encyclopedia, available from http://en.wikipedia.org/wiki/Abu_Muhammad_Asem_al-Maqdisi; Internet; accessed on 3 March 2008.

[28] Chris Hellfinger, "The ideological Voices of the Jihadi Movement," *Terrorism Monitor*, Vol. 4, Issue 24, December 14, 2006 (journal on-line), available from http://www.jamestown.org/terrorism/news/article.php?articleid=2370233&printthis=1; Internet; accessed 19 January, 2008, 2-3.

[29] Ibid., 3.

[30] McCants, *Militant Ideology Atlas*, 7.

[31] Ibid., 8.

[32] Ibid., 7.

[33] William McCants, ed. and Project Director, *Militant Ideology Atlas: Research Compendium* (West Point, NY: Combating Terrorism Center, November, 2006), 329.

[34] Ibid., 345 – 346.

[35] Gunaratna, 35.

[36] William McCants, "Origins of Islam and Islamism," in *Terrorism and Political Islam: Origins, Ideologies and Methods – A Counterterrorism Textbook for the New Agent Training Program at the FBI Academy, Quantico, Virginia,* ed. James J.F. Forest (West Point, NY: Combating Terrorism Center, January 2007), 85.

[37] Ibid., 95.

[38] Walid Shoebat, *Why We Want to Kill You: The Jihadist Mindset and How to Defeat It* (United States: Top Executive Media, 2007), 229 – 232.

[39] Ruth Stein, "Fundamentalism, Father and Son, and Vertical Desire," Ideologies of War, Genocide and Terror, 2006 (journal on-line); available at http://ideologiesofwar.com/docs/fundamentalism_stein.htm; Internet; accessed 21 February 2008.

[40] Dr. Goodson, Middle East Lecture, 26 March 2008.

[41] Hussein Abdulwaheed Amin, "The Origins of the Sunni/Shia Split in Islam*," Islam For Today,* (journal on-line); available from http://www.islamfortoday.com/shia.htm; Internet; accessed 12 January 2008.

[42] "Sufi Islam," *Global Security Organization*, available from http://www.globalsecurity.org/military/intro/islam-sufi.htm; Internet; accessed on 23 March 2008.

[43] Dr. Goodson, Middle East Lecture, 26 March 2008.

[44] Harmony Project, *Cracks in the Foundation: Leadership Schisms in Al-Qa'ida 1989 – 2006* (West Point, NY: Combating Terrorism Center, September 2007), 1.

[45] Randall B. Hamoud, *Osama Bin Laden: America's Enemy in His Own Words* (San Deigo, California: Nadeem Publishing, 2005), xxxvi – xxxvii.

[46] Ibid., xxxix.

[47] Bergen, 90-93.

[48] James Phillips, "Somalia and Al-Qaeda: Implications for the War on Terrorism," *The Heritage Foundation Online,* (journal on-line); available from http://www.heritage.org/Research/HomelandSecurity/BG1526.cfm; Internet; accessed on 19 March 2008.

[49] Ibid.

[50] Ibid.

[51] Ibid.

[52] Mark Bowden, *Black Hawk Down: A Story of Modern War* (New York: Atlantic Monthly Press, 1999), 70 – 99.

[53] United Nations Security Council Resolution 837 (Somalia), United Nations, 6 June 1993, available online at http://daccess-ods.un.org/TMP/4771188.html; Internet; accessed on 15 March 2008.

[54] Matt Eversmann and Dan Schilling eds. *The Battle of Mogadishu: Firsthand Accounts from the men of Task Force Ranger* (New York: Ballentine Press, 2006), 1-4.

[55] Hamoud, xliv – xliv.

[56] Evan F. Kohlmann, *Al-Qaida's Jihad in Europe: The Afghan-Bosnian Network* (Oxford, U.K.: Berg, 2004) 24-25.

[57] Ibid. 35-39.

[58] Ibid. 217 – 219.

[59] Osama Bin Laden, *"1996 Fatwa: Declaration of War against the Americans Occupying the Land of the Two Holy Places,"* CBS News transcript; available from H:\Bin Laden's Fatwa 96.htm; internet; accessed on 5 March 2008.

[60] Bruce Hoffman, *Inside Terrorism* (New York: Columbia University Press, 2006), 94-95.

[61] Osama Bin Lade, "Al Qa'ida 1998 Fatwa", CBS News transcript available from H:\Al Qaeda's 1998 Fatwa.htm; internet; accessed on 5 March 2008.

[62] 9/11 Commission , *Executive Summary 9/11 Commission Report,* available from http://www.9-11commission.gov/report/911Report_Exec.pdf; Internet; accessed on 5 December 2007, 4-6.

[63] U.S. State Department, "Attack on USS Cole", *US Info State Government Web Site,* (journal on-line), available from http://usinfo.state.gov/is/international_security/terrorism/uss_cole.html; Internet; accessed on 14 March 2008, 1.

[64] Harmony Project, *Harmony and Disharmony: Exploiting Al-Qa'ida's Organizational Vulnerabilities Executive Summary* (West Point, NY: Combating Terrorism Center, February 2006), 5.

[65] Harmony Project, "AFGP-2002-600048, Translated April 18 2008," in *Harmony and Disharmony: Exploiting Al-Qa'ida's Organizational Vulnerabilities* (West Point, NY: Combating Terrorism Center, February 2006), 3-4.

[66] Ibid.

[67] Ibid., 3-7.

[68] Peter Grier, *"The New Al Qa'ida: Local Franchiser"*, *Christian Science Monitor*, 11 July 2005, (journal on-line); available from http://www.csmonitor.com/2005/0711/p01s01-woeu.html; Internet; accessed on 12 March 2008.

[69] Harmony Project, "AFGP-2002-000080 Organization, translated 14 Feb 2006," in *Harmony and Disharmony: Exploiting Al-Qa'ida's Organizational Vulnerabilities* (West Point, NY: Combating Terrorism Center, February 2006), 3-4.

[70] Gunaratna, 73–75.

[71] Harmony Project, "AFGP-2002-600048 Al-Qa'ida Bylaws, translated 18 April 2002," in *Harmony and Disharmony: Exploiting Al-Qa'ida's Organizational Vulnerabilities* (West Point, NY: Combating Terrorism Center, February 2006), 5-7.

[72] Harmony Project, "AFGP-2002-000080 Interior Organization, translated 14 Feb 2006," in *Harmony and Disharmony: Exploiting Al-Qa'ida's Organizational Vulnerabilities* (West Point, NY: Combating Terrorism Center, February 2006), 7-10.

[73] Harmony Project, "AFGP-2002-000078 Al-Qa'ida's Goals and Structures, translated 14 Feb 2006), in *Harmony and Disharmony: Exploiting Al-Qa'ida's Organizational Vulnerabilities* (West Point, NY: Combating Terrorism Center, February 2006), 1.

[74] Ibid., 1-5.

[75] Ibid., 5-6.

[76] Ibid., 6–7.

[77] Ibid., 7-8.

[78] Harmony AFGP-2002-600048, 24 -28.

[79] Rand Project Air Force, *Beyond Al-Qaeda Part 1: The Global Jihadist Movement* (California: Rand Corporation, 2006), 25.

[80] Stephen Ulph, "Al Qaeda's Strategy until 2020", *Terrorism Focus,* The Jamestown Organization, Vol. II, Issue, 6, 17 March 2005 (journal on-line) available from http://www.jamestown.org/publications_details.php?volume_id=410&issue_id=3267&article_id=2369441; Internet; accessed on 18 March 2008.

[81] Ibid.

[82] Stephen Ulph, "New Online Book Outlines Al-Qaeda's Military Strategy" *Terrorism Focus,* The Jamestown Foundation, Vol. II, Issue 6, 17 March 2005 (journal on-line) available from http://www.jamestown.org/print_friendly.php?volume_id=410&issue_id=3267&article_id=2369442; Internet; accessed 5 February 2008.

[83] Abu Bakr Naji, *The Management of Savagery: The Most Critical Stage Through which the Umma Will Pass*, trans. William McCants, (Massachusetts: Olin Institute for Strategic Studies, Harvard University, 23 May 2006), 5.

[84] Rand Project Air Force, 30–33.

[85] "Official Source names two Al-Muhayya Compound Bombers – Saudi Arabia," *Saudi Arabian Saudi Arabia Market Information Resource and Directory*, 1 Dec 2003 (newspaper on-line); available from http://www.saudinf.com/main/y6423.htm; Internet; accessed 3 December 2007.

[86] Rand Project Air Force, 33-35.

[87] Naji, 6-9.

[88] Ibid., 9-11.

[89] Sarah E. Zahal, *The Military Strategy of Global Jihad*, Strategic Research Project (Carlise Barracks: U.S. Army War College, 30 March 2007), 7.

[90] Rand Project Air Force, 13.

[91] Gunaratna, 67-68.

[92] Ibid,, 39.

[93] Sammay Salama, "Unraveling Al-Qa'ida's Target Selection Calculus" in *Terrorism and Political Islam: Origins, Ideologies and Methods – A Counterterrorism Textbook for the New Agent Training Program at the FBI Academy, Quantico, Virginia*, ed. James J.F. Forest (West Point, NY: Combating Terrorism Center, January 2007), 41–44.

[94] John Robb, "4GW – Fourth Generation Warfare," *Global Guerillas*, n.d. (journal on-line); available from http://globalguerrillas.typepad.com/globalguerrillas/2004/05/4gw_fourth_gene.html; Internet; accessed 12 December 2007.

[95] Andrew Black, "Al-Suri's Adaption of Fourth Generation Warfare Doctrine", *Terrorism Monitor,* The Jamestown Organization, Vol. 4, Issue 18, 21 September 2006 (journal on-line); available from http://www.jamestown.org/terrorism/news/article.php?articleid=2370137; Internet; accessed 14 March 2008.

[96] Ibid.

[97] William Gerald Beasley, *The Perry Mission to Japan, 1853-1854*, (New York: Routledge, 2002), 140–146.

[98] Amir Butler, "An Enduring Freedom for the Moros", *The Wisdom Fund*, 15 February 2002 (journal on-line); available from http://www.twf.org/News/Y2002/0215-Moros.html; Internet; accessed on 11 February 2008.

[99] "Kamikaze Compared to Suicide Bombers", *Strategy Page*, 18 March 2008; available from http://www.strategypage.com/htmw/htweap/articles/20080318.aspx; Internet; accessed on 18 March 2008.

[100] Ibid.

[101] Yoram Schweitzer, "Palestinian Suicide Bombing Campaigns as a Dynamic Phenomenon", Online Interview by *Andrei Soldatov*, n.d.; available from http://www.agentura.ru/english/experts/schweitzer/; Internet; accessed on 19 March 2008.

[102] Hafez, 211–214.

[103] Ibid,, 214–219.

[104] Ibid., 218–221.

[105] Ibid., 220–221.

[106] Ibid., 220.

[107] Ibid., 224-226.

[108] International Crisis Group, "Understanding Islamism," in *Terrorism and Political Islam: Origins, Ideologies and Methods – A Counterterrorism Textbook for the New Agent Training Program at the FBI Academy, Quantico, Virginia*, ed. James J.F. Forest (West Point, NY: Combating Terrorism Center, January 2007), 61-62.

[109] Daniel Byman, *The Five Front War: The Better Way to Fight Global Jihad* (Hoboken, N.J.: John Wiley and Sons, 2007), 42.

[110] James J.F. Forest, "Introduction to the study of Terrorism and Counterterrorism," in *Terrorism and Political Islam: Origins, Ideologies and Methods – A Counterterrorism Textbook for the New Agent Training Program at the FBI Academy, Quantico, Virginia*, ed. James J.F. Forest (West Point, NY: Combating Terrorism Center, January 2007), 5–7.

[111] Ibid., 6-8.

[112] Michael Vlahos, *Cultures Mask: War and Change after Iraq* (Laurel, Maryland: Johns Hopkins University Press, 2005),13-17.

[113] Quinton Wiktorowicz, *Islamic Activism: A Social Movement Theory Approach* (Bloomington, Indiana: Indiana University Press, 2004), 12–16.

[114] Ibid., 16-20.

[115] International Crisis Group, 59.

[116] Ibid.

[117] 1st BCT-10th Mountain Division, (Unclassified) Lessons Learned from OIF V 2005 – 2006.

[118] 9/11 Commission Report. The Commission uncovered evidence suggesting that between eight and ten of the fourteen "muscle" hijackers, or those designated to gain control of the four 9/11 aircraft and subdue the crews, had passed through Iran in the period from October 2000 to February 2001. Also, Commission investigators discovered that Iran had a history of

allowing Al-Qa'ida members to enter and exit Iran across the Afghan border. This practice dated back to October 2000, with Iranian officials issuing specific instructions to their border guards—in some cases not to put stamps in the passports of al-Qaeda personnel—and otherwise not harass them and to facilitate their travel across the frontier.

[119] Dore Gold, "Ties Between Al-Qaeda and Hamas in MidEast are Long and Frequent," *The San Francisco Chronicle,* 5 March 2006 (newspaper on-line); available from http://www.sfgate.com/cgi-bin/article.cgi?file=/chronicle/archive/2006/03/05/INGERHG75F1.DTL; Internet; accessed on 12 March 2008.

[120] Carl von Clausewitz, *On War,* , ed. and trans., Michael Howard and Peter Paret (Princeton, N.J.: Princeton University Press, 1976), 204-209.

[121] Antulio J. Echevarria II, "Clausewitz's Center of Gravity: Changing Our Warfighting Doctrine – Again!", *US Army War College Strategic Studies Institute* (Carlisle Barracks, PA: n.p., September 2002), 10-11.

[122] Ibid., 12.

[123] Gabriel Weimann, "WWW.terrornet: How Modern Terrorism uses the Internet," *United States Institute of Peace* (Washington, D.C,: n.p., March, 2004), 1.

[124] Ibid,, 2–9.

[125] Muhammad Mustafa Azami *Studies in Hadith Methodology and Literature*, (University of Souther California: n.p., n.d.) available from http://www.usc.edu/dept/MSA/fundamentals/hadithsunnah/; Internet; accessed on 23 March 2008.

[126] Cracks in the Foundation, 1-2.

[127] Ibid., 2-3.

[128] PEW Attitudes Project, "Unease With Major World Powers," *PEW Global Attitudes Project*, June 26, 2007; available from http://pewglobal.org/reports/display.php?ReportID=256; Internet; accessed on 11 February 2008.

[129] Bergen, 90-94.

[130] Bergen, 67-69.

[131] Cracks in the Foundation, 10 -11.

[132] Ibid., 11.

[133] Harun Yahya, *Islam Denounces Terrorism* (England: Amal Press, March 2002),10.

[134] Ibid., 17.

[135] Jean-Charles Brisard and Damien Martinez, *Zarqawi: The New Face of Al-Qaeda* (New York: Otherpress, 2005), 1–6.

[136] Ibid., 7-16.

[137] Ibid., 33.

[138] Ibid., 40-51.

[139] Ibid., 70–78.

[140] Ibid., 93.

[141] Jeffrey Pool, "Zarqawi's Pledge of Allegiance to al-Qaeda: From Mu'asker al-Battar Issue 21," *Terrorism Monitor*, The Jamestown Foundation, Vol 2., Issue 24, 16 December 2004 (journal on-line); available from http://jamestown.org/terrorism/news/article.php?articleid=2369020; Internet; accessed on 20 March 2008.

[142] Michael Scheuer, "The al-Zawahiri al-Zarqawi Letter: Al-Qaedas Tactical and Theater of War Concerns," *Terrorism Focus*, The Jamestown Foundation, Vol 2., Issue 21, 14 November 2005 (journal on-line); available from http://www.jamestown.org/terrorism/news/article.php?articleid=2369830; Internet; accessed on 19 march 2008.

[143] Cracks in the Foundation, 70.

[144] Ibid., 71.

[145] Brian Fishman, "After Zarqawi: The Dilemmas and Future of Al Qaeda in Iraq," *The Washington Quarterly*, (Washington, DC: n.p., July 2006), 20–21.

[146] "2005 Amman Bombings," *Wikipedia Encyclopedia*; available from http://en.wikipedia.org/wiki/2005_Amman_bombings; Internet; accessed on 25 February 2008.

[147] Brian Fishman, 23–24.

[148] Ibid,, 19.

[149] Brian Fishman, "The Imaginary Emir: Al-Qa'ida in Iraq's Strategic Mistake," *Combating Terrorism Center Report*, (West Point, New York: Combating Terrorism Center, 18 April 2007), 1.

[150] Ibid,, 2.

[151] Ibid., 2-3.

[152] "In a Force for Iraqi Calm, Seeds of Conflict," *New York Times*, 27 December 2007 (newspaper on-line); available from http://www.nytimes.com/2007/12/23/world/middleeast/23awakening.html?ei=5090&en=93b15c4

31c7f9bbe&ex=1356066000&partner=rssuserland&emc=rss&pagewanted=all; Internet; accessed on 11 January 2008.

[153] Harmony Project, "Al-Qa'ida's (MIS)ADVENTURES in the Horn of Africa," (West Point, New York: Combating Terrorism Center, 2007), 1.

[154] Ibid,, 1-4.

[155] 9/11 Commission Report, 4-5.

[156] Ibid,, 7–20.

[157] Ibid., 20–21.

[158] George W. Bush, *A National Strategy for Combating Terrorism* (Washington, D.C.: The White House, September 2006), 1.

[159] Office of the Under Secretary of Defense for Acquisition, Technology, and Logisitics, *Report of the Defense Science Board Task Force on Strategic Communication* (Washington, D.C.: September 2004), 36–43.

[160] Peter Katona, Michael D. Intriligator, and John P. Sullivan, eds., *Countering Terrorism and WMD: Creating a Global Counter-terrorism Network* (London: Routledge, 2006), 3.

[161] Phillip H. Gordon, "Can the War on Terror Be Won," *Foreign Affairs,* November/December (journal on-line);available from http://www.foreignaffairs.org/20071101faessay86604/philip-h-gordon/can-the-war-on-terror-be-won.html; Internet; accessed 12 March 2008.

[162] Vlahos, 15.

[163] Elisabeth Rosenthal, "Europe East and West, Wrestles with falling Birthrates" *International Herald Tribune Europe*, 3 September 3 2006 (newspaper on-line); available from http://www.iht.com/articles/2006/09/03/news/birth.php; Internet; accessed on 15 March 2008.

[164] "7 July 2005 London Bombings," *Wikipedia Encyclopedia*, available from http://en.wikipedia.org/wiki/7_July_2005_London_bombings; Internet; accessed on 5 March 2008.

[165] "11 March 2004 Madrid Train Bombings," *Wikipedia Encyclopedia*, available from http://en.wikipedia.org/wiki/11_March_2004_Madrid_train_bombings; Internet; accessed on 5 March 2008.

[166] Dana Dillon, "The Civilian Side of the War on Terror," *Policy Review No. 145*, (October/November 2007), 35–38

[167] Jarret Brachman, "High Tech Terror: Al-Qaedas use of New Technology," in *Terrorism and Political Islam: Origins, Ideologies and Methods – A Counterterrorism Textbook for the New Agent Training Program at the FBI Academy, Quantico, Virginia*, ed. James J.F. Forest (West Point, NY: Combating Terrorism Center, January 2007), 313.

[168] George W. Bush, *National Security Strategy of the United States* (Washington, D.C.: The White House, 2006), Introduction.

[169] Ibid.

[170] Daniel Byman, "Six Years Later: Innovative Approaches to Defeating Al Qaeda," (Washington, D.C.: Brookings Institution, 20 February 2008), 6–9; available from http://brookings.edu/testimony/2008/0214_al_qaeda_byman.aspx?p=11; Internet; accessed on 10 March 2008.

[171] Harmony Project, Militant Ideology Atlas, 6.

[172] Ibid., 6.

[173] Ibid., 10–11.

[174] J. Michael Waller, *Fighting the War of Ideas Like a Real War* (Washington: Institute of World Politics Press, 2007), 66.

[175] Ibid.

[176] Michael Vlahos, *Two Enemies: Non-State Actors and Change in the Muslim World* (Laurel, Maryland: Johns Hopkins University Press, November 2003), 5.

[177] Ibid., 5-6.

[178] Jarrett Bracham, "Leading Egyptian Jihadist Sayyid Imam Renounces Violence" *The Sentinal, Vol I, Issue 1* (West Point, New York: Combating Terrorism Center, December, 2007), 12.

[179] Ibid., 12–13.

[180] Ibid., 13–14.

[181] *Al-Azhar Mosque and University, Cairo Egypt*; Available from http://www.sacred-destinations.com/egypt/cairo-al-azhar-university.htm; Internet; accessed on 20 March 2008.

[182] Mohammed Khalil, "Interview with Sheikh Mohammed Sayyed al-Tantawi, the Grand Imam of Al-Azhar Mosque", *WebIslam*, November, 2006; available from http://english.webislam.com/?idt=344; Internet; accessed on 19 March 2008.

[183] Dore Gold, "Ties between al Qaeda and Hamas in Mideast are long and frequent: It shouldn't be any surprise that the two groups share ideology", *San Francisco Chronicle*, 5 March 5 2006 (newspaper on-line); available from http://www.sfgate.com/cgi-bin/article.cgi?file=/chronicle/archive/2006/03/05/INGERHG75F1.DTL; Internet; accessed on 19 March 2008.

[184] Eban Kaplan, "The Al-Qaeda-Hezbollah Relationship", *Council on Foreign Relations*, 14 August 2006, 1; available from http://www.cfr.org/publication/11275/; Internet; accessed on 12 March 2008.

[185] Ibid., 2.

[186] Waller, 129–131.

[187] "The Amman Message Summary," *The Official Amman Message English Website*; available from http://ammanmessage.com/; Internet; accessed on 21 March 2008.

[188] Waller, 130–132.

[189] Ibid., 130.

[190] Jarret Brachman and William McCants, eds., *Stealing Al'Qaid's Playbook* (West Point, new York: Combating Terrorism Center, 2007), 1– 2.

[191] Ibid., 4–5.

[192] Ibid., 5.

[193] Salama, 49–51.

[194] Jenkins, "New Age of Terrorism," 62.

[195] Brian Michael Jenkins, *Unconquerable Nation: Knowing our Enemy Strengthening Ourselves* (Santa Monica C.A.: Rand 2006), 125–128.

[196] Craig Whitlock, "Why The West can't infiltrate al-Qaida," *The Washington Post*, 20 March 2008 (newspaper on-line); available from http://www.msnbc.com/id/23718506; Internet; accessed on 2 March 2008.

[197] Joseph Rehak, *Discrete Operations in support of Global Counterinsurgency Operations*, Strategy Research Project (Carlisle Barracks: U.S. Army War College, 19 March 2007), 5.

[198] Ken Tovo, *From the Ashes of the Phoenix: Lessons for Contemporary Counterinsurgency Operations*, Strategy Research Project (Carlisle Barracks: U.S. Army War College, 18 March 2005), 1-3.

[199] Ibid.

[200] Rachel Ehrenfeld, PhD., Interviewed by Jamie Glazov on "Funding Evil", *Front Page Magazine,* 15 January 2004; available from http://www.benadorassociates.com/article/1220; Internet; accessed on 15 March 2008.

[201] Shoebat, 6.

[202] Ambassador Cofer Black, "Testimony Before the House International Relations Committee, Subcommittee on International Terrorism,: *United States Congress*, 1 April 2004; available from http://www.state.gov/s/ct/rls/rm/2004/31018.htm; Internet; accessed on 19 march 2008.

[203] Ibid.

[204] Rachel Ehrenfeld, Interview by Eve Harrow, Israeli Arutz TV Channel 7 during the Jeruselem Conference, 20 February 2008; available from http://www.youtube.com/watch?v=_5M71vzPnps; Internet; accessed on 12 March 2008.

[205] Ibid.

[206] Ibid.

[207] Shoebat, 68.

[208] "Saudi Arabia's Curriculum of Intolerance: With Excerpts from Saudi Ministry of Education Textbooks for Islamic Studies: Executive Summary," *Center for Religious Freedom of Freedom House* (Washington, D.C,: Freedom House, 2006), 1–4.

[209] Michael Silverberg, "Wahhabism in the American Prison System," 6 May 2006; available from http://www.jfednepa.org/mark%20silverberg/wahhabi_america.html; Internet; accessed on 21 March 2008.

[210] Ibid.

[211] U.S. Department of State, "U.S. National Strategy for Public Diplomacy and Strategic Communication," (Washington D.C.: State Department, June 2007), 4–5.

[212] Waller, 28.

[213] Ibid,, 35–50.

[214] Mark Lynch, "Al Qaeda's Media Strategy," in *Terrorism and Political Islam: Origins, Ideologies and Methods – A Counterterrorism Textbook for the New Agent Training Program at the FBI Academy, Quantico, Virginia*, ed. James J.F. Forest (West Point, NY: Combating Terrorism Center, January 2007), 71.

[215] Raphael Patai, *The Arab Mind* (New York: Hatherleigh Press, 2002, 285–286.

[216] Jacquelyn K. Davis PhD., and Charles M. Perry PhD., eds., *Rethinking the War on Terror: Developing a Strategy to Counter Extremist Ideologies* (Washington, D.C.: Defense Threat Reduction Agency Working Group, March 2007), 8.

[217] Brackman and McCants, 21.

[218] John D. Negroponte, Deputy Secretary of State, "U.S. Policy Options in Post-Election Pakistan" *Written Testimony before the Senate Foreign Relations Committee*, 28 February 2008; available from http://www.state.gov/s/d/2008/101616.htm; Internet; accessed on 23 March 2008.

[219] "Hamas Charter (1988)," *Palestine Center;* available from http://www.palestinecenter.org/cpap/documents/charter.html; Internet; accessed on 21 march 2008.

[220] Jenkins, "New Age of Terrorism," 39.